LATIN AMERICAN HISTORICAL DICTIONARIES SERIES

Edited by A. Curtis Wilgus

Historical Dictionary
of
HAITI

by

Roland I. Perusse

Latin American Historical Dictionaries, No. 15

The Scarecrow Press, Inc.
Metuchen, N.J.   1977

REF
F
1913
P47

Library of Congress Cataloging in Publication Data

Perusse, Roland I
  Historical dictionary of Haiti.

  (Latin American historical dictionaries ; no. 15)
  Bibliography: p.
  1. Haiti--Dictionaries and encyclopedias.
I. Title.
F1913.P47   972.94'003   76-30264
ISBN 0-8108-1006-9

Dedicated to the wonderful people of Haiti in the fervent hope that their future will be much happier than their past.

EDITOR'S FOREWORD

In his Introduction Professor Perusse has used
many adjectives to give the reader a picture of the country which occupies the western portion of the island of
Hispaniola. I can add little more by way of description
except to say that Haiti throughout its recorded, often
violent history has remained "picturesque" in every
meaning of that word. And the present concise dictionary attests to this fact. As in the case of other com-
pilers of volumes in this series, Dr. Perusse was
asked to select arbitrarily the material for inclusion,
keeping in mind that he was not preparing an encyclo-
pedia but a comprehensive, balanced and logical dictionary.

Roland I. Perusse (known to his friends as RIP)
has had a most interesting and active career, embrac-
ing teaching and administrative academic positions, can-
didacy for a seat in United States Congress, public relations for business and government (including the Com-
monwealth of Puerto Rico and the United States High
Commission in Frankfurt), association with UNESCO
and the United Nations, a career in the United States
Foreign Service, 1950-1962, and work with the National
Security Council and with national defence in general.
He was an officer in the U.S. Army and carried on
consultant activities for the military and for the State
Department in France and Germany.

Born in Springfield, Mass., in 1921, Dr. Perusse
was educated at American University, the Foreign Service Institute, the University of Wisconsin, New York
University, and the Sorbonne. He is a much sought
after authority on Latin America, and especially the
Caribbean, and he has lectured in English, Spanish,
French and German at colleges and universities in the

United States, the West Indies and Europe, often accompanied by his attractive Panamanian wife. He has written and published several books and many articles in his favorite fields of economics, political science, diplomacy and history. He has participated with prepared papers in several national and international conferences. As an authority on the Caribbean his opinion is accepted with assurance. In 1973 he organized the Caribbean Studies Association at the Inter-American University of Puerto Rico at Hato Rey, where he has served as director of the Latin American Program and as professor of political science.

A number of honors have come to Dr. Perusse, including citations, certificates, and society memberships. The "Legion of Merit" (signed by General Eisenhower) was awarded to him in 1945 by the Military Intelligence Service of the U.S. Army.

In this brief Foreword I am happy to welcome my friend and colleague in Puerto Rico as a contributor to the Dictionary Series.

A. Curtis Wilgus
Emeritus Director
School of Inter American Studies
University of Florida

vi

CONTENTS

vii

INTRODUCTION

Perhaps no people have had such a tragic, turbulent yet utterly fascinating history as the people who have inhabited the small corner of the world presently known as Haiti. This area has been populated by three principal races (Indians, whites and blacks) and governed by three sovereignties (Spain, France and the Republic of Haiti). The people who have lived there have been victims of droughts, hurricanes, ignorance, disease, oppression, superstition, invasion, war, revolution, massacres, genocide, slavery, forced labor, exploitation, discrimination, corruption, cruelty, treachery, injustice, hypocricy, dishonesty, intervention and neglect. The Haitian example of man's inhumanity to man has seldom been surpassed anywhere in the world. The first Latin American nation to achieve independence, it is now the last on the scale of social and economic development.

Yet Haiti was once the wealthiest colony on the globe. Its pomp and nobility rivaled that of the courts of Europe. Its history is also replete with acts of bravery, heroism, kindness and sacrifice. Its achievements in art, music, dance and literature are truly phenomenal, especially in the context of extremely adverse conditions. Its culture is a vivacious mix of African and Gallic that permeates all aspects of daily life--speech, worship, customs, artistic expression, etc. Amid poverty, there is an abundance of color and creativity.

This dictionary is designed as an aid in the study of Haiti--the land and its people, their history, politics, government, culture and welfare. Its main utility will be as a reference volume to assist in the comprehension of important terms and names encountered during the perusal of other material. An effort has been made to keep definitions short and pertinent. If the definition, description or short discussion stimulates interest in exploring the subject at greater length, the reader can turn to the bibliography and bibliographical essay at the end of the book for leads on further investigation.

Since this is an English-language dictionary, meant to be used principally by English speakers, the English word rather than the French, Spanish or Creole term is usually entered, for example, "freedman" rather than "affranchi." But if the foreign word is common in English usage, it is generally cross-referenced, for example, "AFFRANCHI see FREEDMAN." Exceptions to this rule are words that would be difficult or awkward to translate, for example, "arrondissement," or foreign words that have been accepted as part of the English vocabulary, for example, "Amis des Noirs." In such cases the French, Spanish or Creole article is usually dropped, for example, "Amis des Noirs" instead of "Les Amis des Noirs," except when the article is obviously an integral part of the name, as in "Les Cayes."

Many persons are listed with only one name. This is due neither to oversight or inadequate research but rather to the fact that the person possessed only one name, as was frequently the case a few centuries ago, especially among persons of common birth.

Hopefully this volume will aid in some small way to an understanding of this much-maligned Caribbean nation and open some doors that may lead to a more pleasant and satisfying future.

Roland I. Perusse
September 1976
Hato Rey, Puerto Rico

x

CHRONOLOGY

1492   Discovery of what is now Hispaniola by Christopher Columbus and the establishment of La Navidad as the first European settlement in the New World.

1496   The Indian chief, Caonabo, is captured and sent as prisoner to Spain.

1500   Bobadilla succeeds Columbus as governor of Hispaniola.

1504   The Spaniards capture and execute Anacaona, widow of Caonabo.

1509   Columbus' son, Diego, is appointed governor of Hispaniola.

1553   The village of Yaguna (later rebuilt as Port-au-Prince) is destroyed by the French pirate, François Le Clerc.

1625   French and British pirates establish themselves on Turtle Island.

1641   Buccaneers become established on the northwestern shores of Hispaniola.

1664   Louis XIV of France lays claim to settlements on the western shores of Hispaniola and places them under the control of the French West India Company.

1697   The Treaty of Ryswick granted France title to the territory west of the Spanish zone of in-

fluence on Hispaniola, in other words, to the
territory presently known as Haiti.

1749   Port-au-Prince is founded by French settlers.

1777   The Treaty of Aránjuez delineated the boundary
        between Saint-Dominique and the Spanish por-
        tion of Hispaniola.

1784   The French recognize the independence of the
        maroons (escaped slaves) in Haiti.

1788   The society, Amis des Noirs, is established in
        Paris.

1790   A colonial assembly, convened by white planters
        and petit blancs in St. Marc, arrogates the
        power of France in the colony of Saint-Dom-
        inique. The assembly was dissolved two years
        later.

1791   The beginning of the slave rebellion, on the
        night of August 14, 1791.

1793   French Commissioner Sonthonax proclaims free-
        dom for the slaves of Saint-Dominique. The
        Spanish invade Saint-Dominique, followed by
        the British.

1794   At Fort Dauphine, 800 white planters are mas-
        sacred by their black slaves.

1795   The Treaty of Basle is signed by which Spain
        ceded the eastern part of Hispaniola to France.

1798   The British sign a secret agreement with Tous-
        saint L'Ouverture ending five years' occupation
        of parts of Saint-Dominique.

1799   The Heads of Regulations are signed between the
        United States and Saint-Dominique. The War
        of Knives begins between the mulattoes and the
        blacks.

1800   Toussaint L'Ouverture gains control of Saint-
        Dominique.

1801   Haiti promulgates its first constitution, though
        still nominally under French sovereignty.

1802   The French arrive at Saint-Dominique with 20,000
        men and commence a campaign to subdue the
        colony.

1803   Toussaint L'Ouverture dies in a French prison.
        The last French troops leave Saint-Dominique
        on December 4, marking the colony's first day
        of true freedom and independence.

1804   The Act of Independence of Haiti is signed on
        January 1 in the city of Gonaïves.   General
        Dessalines assumes the position of governor-
        general for life.

1805   Haiti promulgates its first constitution as an in-
        dependent nation.

1806   Emperor Jacques Dessalines is assassinated.

1807   Henri Christophe proclaims himself President of
        northern Haiti.

1811   Christophe proclaims himself King of the North.

1820   King Henri Christophe commits suicide.

1821   Haiti occupies eastern Hispaniola.

1825   France formally grants Saint-Dominique (Haiti)
        its independence.

1826   The Rural Code is promulgated.

1844   The Dominican Republic overthrows Haitian rule.

1855   Haiti launches an unsuccessful campaign against
        the Dominican Republic.

1915 U. S. forces land in Haiti. A treaty is signed to regulate terms of the occupation. Forced labor is re-instituted.

1918 A new constitution is adopted on the U. S. model. Forced labor is discontinued.

1929 Haitian peasants are massacred by U. S. marines at Marchaterre.

1934 U. S. marines are withdrawn from Haiti, ending 19 years of occupation.

1937 The Dominican Republic massacres 20,000 Haitian cane cutters in the western provinces of the Dominican Republic.

1944 The University of Haiti is established.

1957 François Duvalier is elected President of Haiti.

1963 The United States terminates its foreign aid program in Haiti.

1971 President-for-Life François Duvalier dies and is succeeded by his son, Jean-Claude. The Peligré Dam is inaugurated.

1974 U. S. foreign aid to Haiti is resumed.

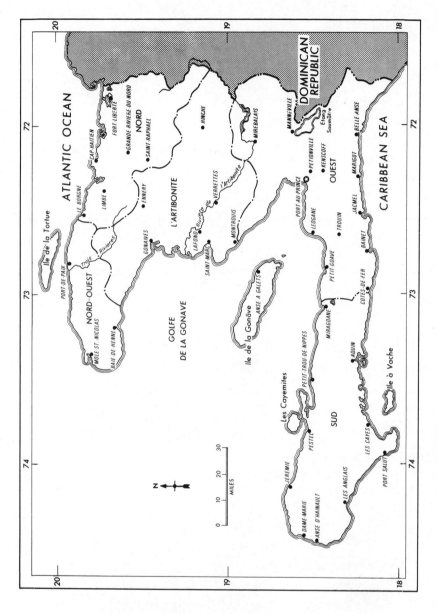

From the <u>Area Handbook for Haiti</u>, U.S. Government
Printing Office, 1973, p. 8.

THE DICTIONARY

ACAAU.   The name of a peasant of the southern peninsula of Haiti who led the Piquets War of 1843.

ACANSAN.   A Nigerian and Dahomean term for balls of
cooked cornmeal.   These are used in Haiti both
for human consumption and for offerings to voodoo
gods.

ACERO D'HAITI.   A semi-autonomous steel company
created in 1791 with joint state and private participation to regulate the production of all metallic
products for construction and consumer use.

AÇON   see   ASON

ACTION DE GRACE.   A Catholic ritual which always
precedes a voodoo ceremony.   Depending upon the
occasion, the "action de grâce" can vary in length
from one or two litanies and a few prayers to an
entire afternoon of worship.

ADJANIKON.   A male assistant in the voodoo cult.
Also called unjankon.

ADMINISTRATIVE COUNCIL.   The elected administrative agency of a rural section, according to the
Rural Code of Haiti.   However, no such councils
function in Haiti at the present time.

ADORATION.   Song sung at ceremonies for the dead.
Also, the term applied to such ceremonies, at
which offerings are made in coins, which are kept
by the person officiating (usually a "prêt' savan'")
as a fee for his services.

1

AFFRANCHI   see   FREEDMEN

AGE.   Haitian Adjutant General sent by Toussaint L'Ou-
    verture in May 1800 with 300 white soldiers to
    assume authority over Santo Domingo.   The Span-
    ish stalled for time, however, and Agé was forced
    to return to Haiti with his troops without accom-
    plishing his mission.

AGRICULTURAL COUNCIL.   A communal advisory group
    made up of the principal farmers and landowners
    of each section.

AGWE WOYO.   Voodoo god of the sea.   His son is
    Agweto Woyo and his daughter Agweta Woyo.

AILHAUD, JEAN-ANTOINE.   One of the three commis-
    sioners sent by France to Saint-Dominique in 1792
    to restore order in the colony.   The other two
    were Léger Félicité Sonthonax and Etienne Polverel.
    Sonthonax quickly pushed Ailhaud into obscurity
    while Polverel assumed a secondary position.

AMIS DES NOIRS.   The name of a French society dedi-
    cated to the abolition of slavery.   It was estab-
    lished in Paris on February 19, 1788.   At first
    gradualist in nature, concerned primarily with
    mulatto equality, it became more radical during
    the French Revolution.   Léger Félicité Sonthonax,
    French Commissioner to Saint-Dominique from
    1792 to 1794, was closely associated with the
    Amis des Noirs and personified the radical wing of
    the French Revolution.

ANACAONA.   Widow of the Indian chief, Caonabo, who
    governed the Indian Kingdom of Xaragua.   She was
    a beautiful woman, possessed of the art of lulling
    away the cares of her followers by extemporizing
    native songs of which they were so fond.   Like
    her husband, she became a victim of Spanish
    tyranny.   In 1504, under the pretext of collecting
    tribute due the Court of Spain, the Spanish gover-
    nor, Nicholás Ovando, left for Xaragua with 300

foot soldiers and 70 cavalrymen.   In pursuance of
Anacaona's instructions, the Indians everywhere
gave him a friendly welcome.   Festivities were
held in honor of the Spaniards.   On one such
occasion, on a given signal agreed upon before-
hand, the Spanish pounced upon the innocent Indians
and began to slaughter them.   Anacaona was taken
prisoner and sentenced to death in a mock trial.
Neither her beauty nor her art could excite the
compassion of her conquerors and she was hanged.

ANSE A GALETS.   Small village on the island of
    Gonâve.

ANSE D'HAINAULT.   Small coastal village on the eastern
    extremity of the southern peninsula of Haiti.

AQUIN.   Small town on the southern coast of Haiti.

ARANJEZ, TREATY OF.   Treaty which delineated the
    boundary between the French and Spanish portions
    of Hispaniola in 1777.

ARAWAK.   The name given to the Indians which in-
    habited Haiti and the island of Hispaniola at the
    time of Columbus' arrival.   Within a few years,
    they were completely decimated by the Spaniards.

ARCAHAYE CONFERENCE.   Conference of black and
    mulatto generals that recognized Dessalines as
    leader of the resistance to France.   The confer-
    ence adopted a red and blue flag as its banner
    and declared for Haitian independence.

ARDOUIN, BEAUBRUN.   Foremost Haitian geographer.
    His "La Géographie de l'Ile d'Haiti," first pub-
    lished in 1856, is one of the early authoritative
    works on Haitian geography.

ARNOUX, MAX.   One of Haiti's better known contem-
    porary artists.

ARRET.   A charm thought to protect the wearer against

evil. Also called a garde or drogue.

ARRONDISSEMENT. Unit of local government in Haiti. Five departments are divided into arrondissements, which in turn are divided into communes.

ART CENTER. A center for artistic training and exhibition in Port-au-Prince, founded in 1944 by the American painter, Dewitt Peters.

ARTIBONITE. A funnel-shaped area of about 300 square miles in the north of Haiti, north of the Chaine de Mateaux; also the name of the river flowing through this region.

The Artibonite is often called the breadbasket of Haiti because of its fertile soil. The Artibonite River rises in the Cibao mountains and empties into the Gulf of Gonâve, near Grande-Saline. It drains about 1,581,500 acres of land.

Extensive efforts have been made in the past to enlarge the productive area of the Artibonite through irrigation. Near the coast, the soil is too alkaline for intensive cultivation.

ASAGWE. A dance saluting the voodoo gods.

ASON. Dried gourd with beads on the outside, used by voodoo priests and priestesses. It may also be strung with the dried vertebrae of snakes.

ASOTOR. Voodoo drum which sometimes reaches the height of nine feet. It is cut from a single tree trunk, which is hollowed and dried.

ASSEMBLE NATIONAL see NATIONAL ASSEMBLY

AUGUSTE, TANCREDE. President of Haiti from August 8, 1912, to May 2, 1913. He died by poison on the latter date.

AUGUSTE, TOUSSAINT. Contemporary Haitian artist, renowned for the symmetry of his paintings.

AVALOU. A voodoo dance of supplication, characterized by vigorous arm and shoulder movements. Also pronounced "yanvalou" or "yenvalo."

AZACCA. Voodoo god of agriculture. He is said to be peasant-like and to be a hard worker.

AZETO   see   LOUP GAROU

- B -

BACALOU (Bakulou). Evil voodoo spirit which feeds on human flesh.

BACCALAUREAT. Certificate awarded after seven years of secondary school education.

BAGUETTE. Drumstick.

BAIE-DE-HENNE. Small village on the southern coast of the Department of the Northwest.

BAIGNEUR DES MORTS. Man or woman (of the same sex as the dead person) who bathes the body and prepares it for a funeral.

BAINET. Small town on the southern coast of Haiti.

BAKA. According to voodoo belief, an evil spirit, usually in the form of an animal, which does harm according to instructions imparted by the person who has dispatched it.

BAL. Creole term for any dance of European origin.

BAMBOCHE. Literally, a "spree." It is the customary way of family celebration of weddings, birthdays, and other ceremonial occasions. It is similar to voodoo but is not presided over by voodoo priests.

BANDA. A sexual dance characterized by hip gyrations, common at funeral ceremonies and carnival.

BANDE DE MACHOIRE. A cloth placed under the chin and over the head of a dead person, to hold the jaw in place. It is usually removed when the body is placed in a coffin.

BANQUE NATIONAL see NATIONAL BANK

BAPTISTE, JOHN. Leader of a slave rebellion in Saint-Dominique in 1791. He was killed in its early stages.

BARBOT, CLEMENT. Private secretary to François Duvalier during the latter's early years of power. He was the trusted advisor of the president and helped in organizing the secret police. He secretly negotiated with the United States and the Dominican Republic for aid and recognition, should he gain the office of the presidency. As a result, he was arrested and imprisoned by President Duvalier. On release, he went underground, pledging to overthrow the President, who then ordered him shot on sight. He was cornered in a cane field five miles from the capital. Soldiers of the Palace Guard set fire to the field and shot Barbot and nine of his followers as they ran from the fire and smoke.

BARON SAMEDI. According to voodoo belief, a god who lives in the cemetery who is the power behind magic that kills. He is said to control the souls of those who have met death as a result of magic.

BARRIERE. Creole term for "entrance way." The voodoo god, Legba, supposedly guards entrances.

BASILIQUE. A tree whose leaves, according to voodoo belief, are effective in warding off evil spirits. The leaves may also be soaked in water and used for ritual cleansing.

BASSIN. A deep pool in a stream which, according to voodoo belief, serves as the home of various water spirits.

BATTERIE MACONNIQUE. A slow, measured beating
    of drums and clapping of hands near the beginning
    of a voodoo ceremony, meant to open the door to
    the world of voodoo gods.

BATTRAVILLE, BENOIT. Caco chief who led anti-U.S.
    resistance forces into Port-au-Prince on January
    15, 1920.

BAUSSAN, ROBERT. Haitian architect credited with
    Albert Mangones with having brought Haitian arch-
    itecture from the classical French style to simpler
    and functional modern international lines.

BAUXITE. An ore from which alumina is refined to
    produce aluminum. Haiti produces about 1 percent
    of the world's bauxite but has significant reserves.
    Bauxite is the country's second most important ex-
    port commodity after coffee.

BEAUVAIS, LOUIS. One of the early leaders of the Hai-
    tian Revolution. He is said to have served in the
    American Revolution at the siege of Savannah. Up-
    on his return to Saint-Dominique, he taught school
    until the outbreak of the Haitian Revolution.

BELAIR, CHARLES. One of Toussaint's most capable
    field commanders. He also served under the
    French general Le Clerc but defected upon the ex-
    ecution of an all-Negro brigade which had mutinied.
    He led his own regiment into the hills to join the
    rebel forces. Bélair had the support of many
    blacks and was considered Toussaint's possible suc-
    cessor until he was captured and executed by Des-
    salines, who considered him a dangerous rival.

BELLE ANSE. Small village on the southern coast of
    Haiti about 30 miles from the border with the Do-
    minican Republic.

BELLEGARDE, DANTES (1877-1966). Editor, diplomat,
    educator and social historian and the author of

about 24 books. He was the last influential figure
in a long line of francophile traditionalists. Bellegarde served as Minister of Public Instruction in
Haiti in 1918. He struggled to improve the Haitian
school system against great odds: apathy, lack of
funds, the spoils system and U.S. interference.

BENOIT, RIGAUD. Contemporary Haitian artist.

BESSE, HENRI. Haitian engineer who supervised the
construction of the Citadelle.

BIASSOU. Early Haitian revolutionary leader. He tried
unsuccessfully to make peace between the blacks
and white French colonialists. Like Toussaint
L'Ouverture, he did military duty with the Spanish
forces of Santo Domingo in their war against
France and their invasion of the North Province of
Saint-Dominique.

BIBLIOTHEQUE DU PETIT HAÏTIEN. Educational com-
pilation in Creole, prepared by Frédéric Doret,
constituting a collection of booklets designed to ed-
ucate the common man.

BIGAUD, WILSON. One of Haiti's best known primitive
painters. One of his most acclaimed works is the
mural, "Miracle at Cana," in the Holy Trinity Cathedral at Port-au-Prince depicting the New Testa-
ment feast in a Haitian setting. His "Earthly Par-
adise" and "Cockfight" are also well known.

BLACK CODE. A French law, promulgated in 1685,
which regulated relations between whites and blacks
in the colonies. Though very discriminatory and
providing for stern disciplinary measures for
slaves, it nonetheless also sought to provide for
their welfare and humane treatment. It stipulated,
for example, that they should be taught the Roman
Catholic faith and be excused from work on Sunday
and religious holidays. These "rights" of the
slaves, however, were generally ignored by their
masters.

BLANCHELANDE.   French Governor of the colony of
Saint-Dominique from 1790 to 1792.   He was responsible for the trial and execution of the early
Haitian revolutionary leader, Vincent Ogé.   Yet
he was opposed by the Colonial Assembly for not
being sufficiently firm with the insurgents.   When
the Jacobins came to power in France, he was de-
ported from Haiti to France, where he was guil-
lotined.

BLANC-PODAN   see   PETIT-BLANC

BOBADILLA.   Successor to Columbus on the island of
Hispaniola.   His treatment of the Indians was most
oppressive, and he was removed after two years
(1500-1502).

BOCOR.   A sorcerer in the religion of voodoo, thought
to be capable of casting a spell, for good or for
evil, on another person.

BOGOTA.   An old automobile.   The term dates from a
period when many used automobiles were imported
from Colombia.

BOIS-CAIMAN OATH.   Oath to fight for freedom till
death, taken on a stormy night of August 14, 1791,
by slave leaders of Plaine du Nord plantations,
which touched off the Haitian Revolution.

BOLIVAR, SIMON.   (1783-1830).   The famous Liberator
of South America, who visited Alexandre Pétion in
southern Haiti in 1816.   Pétion gave Bolívar material support in return for a pledge that he,
Bolívar, would free the slaves of Venezuela and
other areas he might conquer.   Bolívar copied the
Haitian institution of a life-long presidency when
he drew up the Bolivian Constitution of 1826.

BORGELLA, BERNARD.   Mayor of Port-au-Prince and
chairman of a Central Assembly of ten members
who drafted the first Haitian Constitution of 1801.

BORNO, LOUIS (1865-1942). President of Haiti from 1922 to 1930. He was the handpicked choice of the U.S. high commissioner to Haiti, General John H. Russell, and the two governed Haiti together in what has been called a "two-headed dictatorship."

BOSALE. An unclean spirit not yet initiated into the rites of voodoo. Also, a slave who has just arrived from Africa who is not yet "socialized" to the manners and mores of his new environment.

BOUBOU. A sack-like garment worn by the poorer classes in Haiti.

BOUDET, JEAN. French general and division commander during Le Clerc's campaign to subdue the black insurrection in Haiti. Boudet took the city of Port-au-Prince but made little progress in the countryside because of fierce resistance and harassment from the Haitian commander, Dessalines.

BOUKMAN. A huge, muscular man and fugitive slave from Jamaica. He was a voodoo priest who despised whites and was the leader of the slave rebellion of August 22, 1791. He was taken prisoner and beheaded. His head, stuck on the end of a pole, was exposed in the center of Cap-Haïtien (then Cap-Français) with a sign bearing the words, "Head of Boukman, chief of the rebels."

BOYER, JEAN-PIERRE (1787-1850). President of Haiti for Life (March 30, 1818, to March 13, 1843). Boyer reunited the north and south of Haiti and extended Haitian domination over the entire island.
  A mulatto educated in France, Boyer tried to ward off a second invasion by France by granting special trade privileges to the French in return for recognition of Haitian independence. This angered the blacks and led Boyer to adopt stern measures. He was overthrown and exiled by a conspiracy of fellow mulattoes. In the ensuing turmoil the people of Santo Domingo overthrew Haitian rule and re-established the Dominican Republic in eastern Hispaniola.

Boyer's principal achievements were promulgation of a Rural Code to force peasants to work and a treaty with the French by which the latter recognized Haitian independence.

BREADFRUIT. A fruit of the humid lowlands which is baked or boiled into a sticky dough.

BREAK. A sharp change in folk dance step to avoid the hypnotic effect of drums and gourds, also called a "feint."

BREDA PLANTATION. Plantation where Toussaint L'Ouverture served as a slave until 1791. Toussaint became steward of the Bréda Plantation and was favored by its owner, Comte de Noé.

BREDA, TOUSSAINT see TOUSSAINT L'OUVERTURE

BREVET ELEMENTAIRE. Certificate awarded in Haiti after nine years of primary education.

BROUARD, CARL. Haitian poet who wrote in French but in the style and sentiment of the Creole dialect.

BRUNEL, JOSEPH. Agent sent by Toussaint L'Ouverture to Philadelphia in 1798 to negotiate an alliance with Saint-Dominique.

BRUNET. French general who tricked Toussaint into captivity. Toussaint was summoned by Brunet to discuss among other matters destruction on Toussaint's plantation by French troops. Brunet vouched for his safety, and Toussaint proceeded with practically no escort. The black leader was arrested, bound hand and foot, and carried to France aboard a French vessel.

BUCCANEER. Inhabitant of the island of Tortuga in the 17th century. The name comes from the French word, "boucaner," which means "to smoke," and from the French word, "boucan," the grill over which buccaneers smoked their meat. They were a cosmopolitan group, mainly French, who preyed

on Spanish commerce and raided nearby sections
of the main island of Hispaniola, then under Spanish control.
 The buccaneers became established on the northwestern shores of Hispaniola in 1630, thus giving
the French a claim to the western part of the Island.

BULA. The smallest of the three drums used in a voodoo ceremony.

BUTIO. Indian priest at the time of the discovery of
Hispaniola. The Butios were at once soothsayers
and doctors. By tradition and through personal
observation, they knew the medical properties of
many plants.

BUTLER, SMEDLEY D. (1881-1940). U.S. Marine major who became the first commandant of the Haitian
gendarmerie during the U.S. occupation of Haiti.
In theory the gendarmerie was under the command
of the Haitian president, but Butler refused to take
orders from any Haitian. Butler revived the corvée
in Haiti in order to construct a system of roads.
It was abolished again in 1918.

- C -

CABRONNE, LUCKNER. Minister of the Interior in
President Jean-Claude Duvalier's first Cabinet,
from 1971. He went into exile following charges
of corruption.

CACICAT. Early Indian Kingdom in the land presently
known as Haiti.

CACIQUE. Tribal chief of the Indians in the land now
known as Haiti.

CACIQUE ISLAND. A resort area, about half an hour
by automobile from Port-au-Prince. Visitors are
lodged in native huts which have all the amenities
of modern living. The complex was designed by
the architect Robert Baussan.

CACO. A kingmaker. Cacos were peasants who would
    make an agreement with a Haitian presidential as-
    pirant under which, for a certain sum to be paid
    after a successful revolution and the opportunity to
    loot, they would lead an insurrection to place a
    new leader in power. During the U.S. occupation
    of 1915, caco leaders organized an uprising which
    was suppressed by the U.S. Marines after several
    years of guerrilla warfare. This served as a
    deathblow to cacos tactics and aspirations.

CACOS WAR. The "war" begun in 1867 as an alliance
    between peasants and the army. It ended in 1870
    but during the last quarter of the century and un-
    til the U.S. occupation peasant rebellions were the
    principal instrument for the transfer of political
    power in Haiti.

CAILLE. Creole word for "hut."

CAILLE MYSTERES. A hut where voodoo gods are wor-
    shipped.

CALE BASSE. Shells of gourds, which are used for mu-
    sical instruments or kitchenware.

CALIXTE, DEMOSTHENES PETRUS. Commander of the
    Garde d'Haiti following the U.S. occupation, 1915-
    1934. He accepted and followed the U.S. tradition
    of military subordination to civilian control, despite
    the excesses of the president under whom he served.

CAMBEFORT, JOSEPH-PAUL. French commander of the
    Le Cap Regiment deported to France in 1792 by
    French Commissioner Léger Félicité Sonthonax.
    Cambefort was tried by a Jacobin court and acquitted.

CAMIONETTE. A gaily colored truck for carrying pas-
    sengers. A wooden frame is mounted on a chassis
    to construct this public conveyance. There are
    many of these in Haiti, and they are inevitably
    overflowing with their passengers and baggage. In-
    evitably, too, they are given humorous or philoso-

phical names which are painted on the front of the
vehicle.

CANAL, BOISROND. President of Haiti from July 17,
1876, to July 17, 1879. He was the only president
of Haiti to adhere strictly to the Constitution in his
relations with the legislature. Elected as a Liberal after the corrupt regime of Michel Dominique,
he attempted to make the parliamentary system
work. However the two chambers spent so much
time criticizing Canal and trying to assert their
supremacy that he resigned in disgust.

CANARIS. Vessels for storing or transporting water.

CANTAVE, LEON. General in command of the Haitian
armed forces in the late 1950's. He served as a
stabilizing influence to the rapid succession of acting presidents who were unable to govern and to
the political cliques competing for power. Dismissed by President Duvalier, he led an invasion
of Haiti in 1963 at Fort Liberté. He was driven
into the Dominican Republic by Government forces.

CANZO. The second stage of voodoo. Here the "loa,"
or god which has entered the person's spirit, is
tamed and controlled, and the person is eligible to
assist in voodoo ceremonies.

CAONABO. Chief of the Indian Kingdom of Maguana on
the island of Hispaniola who destroyed the Spanish
fortress of La Navidad and killed all its Spanish
inhabitants. He became the leader of Indian opposition to the Spaniards. Under the pretext of making peace, Caonabo was presented with chains and
handcuffs made of iron and polished to glitter like
silver. The unsuspecting Indian admired the irons
and mistaking them for ornaments, he allowed himself to be manacled. He was then carried to Columbus, who kept him prisoner in his own house.
He was sent to Spain in March 1496. According
to one account, the ship foundered and the cacique
was drowned. According to another account, the

Indian leader starved himself to death during the
voyage.

CAPERTON, ADMIRAL W. B. (1855-1941).   Commander
of U.S. naval forces that invaded Haiti in 1915 and
of the U.S. occupation of Haiti (1915-1934).   He
transformed what was meant to be a temporary and
limited intervention at Port-au-Prince into a formal
and unlimited occupation of the entire country.   On
his own initiative he proclaimed the subordination
of Haitian authority to his martial rule.   On his
authority as "Commanding Officer of the Forces of
the United States in Haiti and Haitian waters" and
"in accordance with the law of nations," he declared
himself "invested with the power and responsibility of government in all its functions and
branches."

CAP-FRANÇAIS.   Name for Cap-Haïtien when Haiti was
under French control.   For a short period under
the reign of Henri Christophe, it was called Cap-
Henri.

CAP-HAÏTIEN.   Second largest city of Haiti (pop.
20,000), lying on the northern coast.   It was the
early capital of Haiti and is now the administrative
center of the Department of the North.
    Cap-Haïtien was one of the thriving ports of Hai-
ti before independence.   In the 18th century, U.S.
trade with Cap Français (as it was then called) and
nearby Léogane was second in value only to U.S.
trade with Great Britain.

CAP-HENRI.   Name for Cap-Haïtien under the rule of
King Henri Christophe.

CAPLATA.   A term of ridicule used to characterize a
minor practitioner of magic.

CAPOIX-LA-MORT.   Leader of Haitian resistance to
France in the early 1800's.

CAYES, LES   see   LES CAYES

CEDOR, DIEUDONNE.   One of Haiti's better known contemporary artists.

CENTRAL ASSEMBLY.   Committee of ten, headed by
Bernard Borgella, white mayor of Port-au-Prince,
which drafted Haiti's first constitution in 1801.
The committee was composed of seven whites and
three mulattoes, but was under the control and
dominance of Toussaint L'Ouverture.

CENTRAL PLATEAU.   Area from Montagnes Noir to the
Dominican border.   The largest of Haiti's flatlands,
the plateau has an average elevation of 1,000 feet.
Its soils are useful only for pasturage.

CEREMONY-YAM.   The offering of the first fruits of
the fields to the voodoo gods so that they will again
render the fields productive in the coming season.

CERTIFICATE OF PRIMARY STUDIES (Certificat d'études
primaires).   Certificate awarded in Haiti after six
years of primary education.

CESAR, PHILIPPE.   One of the three commissioners
sent by Toussaint L'Ouverture to negotiate peace
with the mulatto leader, André Rigaud, in 1800.
Rigaud spurned the offer.

CHA-CHA.   Seed-filled calabash used as an instrument
to accompany dance music.

CHAINE DE MATEAU.   A mountain range with a south-
westerly axis extending from the Gulf of Gonâve to
the frontier with the Dominican Republic.

CHAIRO PIE.   A shuffling-type dance performed by
groups during carnival or work projects.

CHAMBER OF DEPUTIES.   Haiti's unicameral legislature, composed of 58 delegates elected for four-
year terms.

CHANDELLE.   A cactus-type plant shaped like a cande-

labra usually grown as property dividers. Its milk
is midly poisonous.

CHARLES, NORMAN ULYSSES. Haitian sculptor who
created the well-known monument to Toussaint
L'Ouverture in the city of Port-au-Prince.

CHARMANT, ALCIUS. Haitian author of a book pub-
blished in 1905 and dedicated to the blacks of Haiti,
which is extremely critical of mulattoes, entitled,
Haiti, vivra-t-elle? Etude sur le préjugé des races;
race noire, race jaune, race blanche, et sur la
Doctrine de Monroe.

CHAVANNES, JEAN-BAPTISTE. Free mulatto who joined forces with Vincent Ogé in 1791 to try to win
rights for the men of their color in Saint-Dominique.
They were unsuccessful and fled to Spanish territory but were returned by the Spanish and broken
on the wheel by the French colonists in Saint-Dominique.

CHEF DE SECTION see CHIEF OF SECTION

CHEF D'ESQUADE. Creole term for the man who calls
together a combite.

CHIEF OF SECTION. Lowest-ranking political-military
figure in rural Haiti.

CHIEFS OF STATE see Appendix

CHRISTOPHE, FERDINAND. Prince of Haiti, the eldest
son of Henri Christophe. The father, desirous that
his son acquire a sound French education, entrusted
him to the care of a French general officer return-
ing to France. He provided funds for the boy's
education and maintenance. Henri Christophe later
learned that the boy was placed in an orphan asy-
lum in Paris, where he died from neglect.

CHRISTOPHE, HENRI (1767-1820). Called the "Civili-
zer," he reportedly fought in Savannah, Georgia,

with the French on the side of the Americans in
the American Revolution. He was president of the
northern part of Haiti from January 1807 to March
1811, then king of the North under the name of
King Henri I until his death on October 8, 1820.

According to an official document, published on
his own order, Christophe was born on the island
of Grenada on October 6, 1767. Some historians
place his birth on the island of St. Kitts, which is
also known as St. Christopher, because of his
name. Some authorities say he was born of free
Negroes, others say his parents were slaves.
What is pretty well established, however, is that
he was a pure-blooded black and that he was a
slave as a young boy. He became the property of
a French naval officer whom he accompanied to
Savannah, Georgia, during the American Revolution.
He finally purchased his freedom and wed his master's daughter.

Christophe, with Toussaint and Dessalines, was
one of the three great black leaders of the Haitian
Revolution. With the removal of Toussaint to
France and the assassination of Dessalines, he was
chosen president of the Haitian Republic in 1806.
However, the office had been so weakened under a
new constitution that he refused to serve and as-
saulted Port-au-Prince with his troops in an effort
to gain full control. He was stopped by Pétion's
forces and retreated to the North, where he set up
his own State of Haiti. The next few years saw
indecisive civil war between the two jurisdictions,
then an armed truce. When Pétion was reelected
president in the South, Christophe had himself proclaimed king in the North. He set up a court and
nobility meant to rival any in Europe. His Palace
of Sans Souci and the fortress Citadelle la Ferriére
are monuments to his striving for pomp and security.

Tall and muscular, Christophe loved ostentation.
As a result of a mutiny, he committed suicide on
October 8, 1820, according to legend with a silver
(or gold) bullet saved for that purpose.

Christophe made everyone work and instituted
military discipline. Agriculture and commerce

were revived and the people in the North enjoyed
a degree of security and stability under his rule
that they had not known for a decade.   But his
autocratic methods finally generated rebellion when
he was weakened by illness and lost his grip on
the masses.

CIGOUAVES.   According to voodoo beliefs, demons with
wolf bodies and human heads especially dangerous
and prone to tear out the sexual organs of men.

CISEAUX.   A dance where feet and legs cross one another in a scissor-like movement.

CITADEL LA FERRIERE.   Often called the "eighth won-
der of the world," the Citadel la Ferrière is a
fort constructed by Henri Christophe during the
period 1804-1817.   According to legend, the construction of this massive mountain-top bastion cost
the lives of from 20,000 to 25,000 slaves.   It was
said that 10,000 soldiers could be housed in the
fortress.   It commands an unrivaled view of the
sea coast and the mountains.   Its walls are up to
12 feet thick.
      Today the fortress lies in ruins.   Its cannon sit
on rotting wooden carriages.   The tropical jungle
has thrown its mantle over the fortifications.   Built
for defense against the French, it was never used
for military purposes.   Christophe's tomb is in a
small rectangular building in the courtyard.

CIVIL TRIBUNAL.   Civil court of the arrondissement
having both primary and appellate juridiction.

CLAIRIN.   Raw white rum popular with the peasants of
Haiti.

CLERVEAUX.   Leader of Haitian resistance against
France in the early 1800's.

CLUB MASSIAC   see   MASSIAC CLUB

COCOMACAQUE.   Club made from a variety of small
coconut tree.

CODE HENRI. A series of laws regulating commerce,
    civil proceedings, the police, agriculture and mili-
    tary affairs, issued by King Henri Christophe in
    1811.

CODE NOIR   see   BLACK CODE

COICOU, MASSILON. Poet and playwright at the turn
    of the 20th century who was among the first to in-
    troduce Creole into the national literature.

COLONIAL ASSEMBLY. An assembly convoked by white
    planters and petit-blancs at Saint-Marc on April 14,
    1790, upon petition to the French National Assembly
    and ostensibly to deal with the internal affairs of
    the colony of Saint-Dominique in the name of
    France.   Fired by the principles of the French
    Revolution, it arrogated unto itself supreme author-
    ity over the colony and promulgated a constitution.
    The Colonial Assembly ignored the King's repre-
    sentatives on the island (the Governor-General and
    other officials) but nevertheless acknowledged alle-
    giance to the French King. It was dissolved in
    1792 by French commissioners sent to Haiti follow-
    ing the French Revolution.

COLONIAL COMMITTEE. The organization of the grands
    blancs of Saint Dominique.   Determined to play a
    role in French governance of the colony, the colo-
    nial committee sent 37 representatives to the French
    Estates General.   This representation was later re-
    duced to six.

COLONS AMERICAINS. Mulatto pressure group in Paris
    in the late 18th century, led by Vincent Ogé and
    Julien Raimond.

COLUMBUS, CHRISTOPHER. Discoverer of Haiti on
    December 2, 1492, on his first voyage to the New
    World.   He established the town and fortress of La
    Navidad in the north as the first European settle-
    ment in the Americas.

COMBITE. A working party of neighbors assembled by
    a small farmer to help in needed work. The vol-
    unteer workers are not paid but receive a liberal
    allowance of food and drink while working, accom-
    panied by singing or the beating of drums. Work
    usually ends in midafternoon but entertainment may
    continue far into the night.

COMMERE. Creole term for godmother.

COMMUNAL COUNCIL. The organ of administration of
    the commune, according to the code of Haiti.

COMMUNE. Unit of local government in Haiti. The
    country is divided into five departments, which are
    divided into arrondissements, which in turn are
    divided into communes.

COMPARET. A round spice cake common to the region
    of Jéremie. The word is a contraction of "Quand
    'ou' [vous] paraître" which means "when you   -
    appear." The cake is served "when you appear."

COMPERE. Creole term for godfather.

CONADEP see NATIONAL COUNCIL FOR PLANNING
    AND DEVELOPMENT

CONCORDAT. Agreement governing the relations be-
    tween Haiti and the Vatican, signed in Rome on
    March 28, 1860.

CONNAISSANCE. Understanding of the meaning and mys-
    teries of the voodoo religion. The hierarachy of
    voodoo practitioners is based on the degree of spir-
    itual understanding and insight into supernatural
    forces that each is believed to possess.

CONSEIL NATIONAL DE DEVELOPPEMENT ET DE
    PLANIFICATION see NATIONAL COUNCIL FOR
    PLANNING AND DEVELOPMENT

CONSTITUTION OF 1801. Haiti's first constitution, pro-

mulgated by Toussaint L'Ouverture after gaining
control of the French colony of Saint-Dominique.
The Constitution made Toussaint governor general
for life, with power to designate his successor.
It abolished slavery and required all males from
14 to 55 years of age to serve in the militia. Ca-
tholicism was recognized as the state religion.

CONSTITUTION OF 1805. Constitution of the Empire of
Haiti under Emperor Jean-Jacques Dessalines. It
provided that all Haitians would assume the generic
name of "black" and forbade foreigner to own
land. Naturalized wives and Poles and Germans
who had deserted to the insurgents were excepted.
It pledged that Haiti "would never undertake any
conquest nor break the peace and internal regime
in foreign colonies. " Freedom of religion was
guaranteed.

CONSTITUTION OF 1806. Constitution creating a republican form of government modeled after England
and the United States. It sought to prevent abuses
of executive power by concentrating significant powers in a Senate.

CONSTITUTION OF 1843. A liberal document which
gave the peasantry the right to vote, abolished the
institution of president-for-life, strengthened legislative prerogatives, instituted trial by jury and established civil control over the military. It was
ignored by then-President Hérard, who chose to
rule by force.

CORPS LEGISLATIF. The legislature in the early years
of the Republic of Haiti.

CORRECTIONAL TRIBUNAL. The criminal court of the
arrondissement, having both original and appellate
jurisdiction.

CORRIGOLE, CHARLES. Black commander who continued to resist French forces in Haiti, even after
the surrender of Toussaint L'Ouverture and Dessalines.

CORVEE.   Forced labor.   In 1915, U.S. occupation authorities reinstituted the corvée in Haiti.   The re-
quirement was three days' labor a year on the
roads in the peasant's home district.   It was ordered discontinued on October 1, 1918.

COTES-DE-FER.   Small town on the southern coast of
Haiti.

COTUBANA.   Indian chief of the Kingdom of Higuey in
eastern Hispaniola at the beginning of the 16th century.   He was taken prisoner by the Spanish and
hanged.

COUNCIL OF STATE.   An appointed group of advisors
to the President of Haiti.

COURT OF CASSATION.   The highest court in Haiti.   It
is composed of a President, Vice President and ten
judges.   It usually functions in two chambers of
five judges each, but when it hears appeals and
constitutional issues, it functions as a whole.

COUVERT SEC   see   MANGE SEC

CREOLE.   The native language of Haiti, which is spoken
by nearly all of the population in preference to
French, which is the official language and is spoken
only by the elite.   Creole is a combination of African dialects, French, Spanish and a little English
and Portuguese.   Also, a term used to characterize
those born on the island.

CRETE-A-PIERROT.   An important supply depot and
gateway to the Grands Cabos Mountains.
When French General Le Clerc invaded the colony of Saint-Dominique in 1802, Toussaint L'Ouverture pulled his forces in the north behind this stra-
tegic pass and fortress.   Twelve hundred blacks
held out for a month against attacks by 12,000
Frenchmen.   Between bombardments, the blacks
sang patriotic songs of the French Revolution, completely demoralizing the French troops, who began
questioning their role in Saint-Dominique.   The

fortress fell to the French but the price was high: 2000 men and a spectacular demonstration of the courage and fighting capacity of ex-slaves.

CRYPLOSTEGIA. A latex-producing vine. During World War II, the SHADA (Société Haitienne-Américaine de Développement) attempted large-scale cultivation of cryplostegia as a possible source of latex, a scarce commodity during the war, but the vine produced an insufficient amount of latex to make the effort worthwhile.

CUL-DE-SAC. Lowland area of about 150 square miles in the south between the Chaîne de Mateaux and the Massif de la Selle.

CULTIVATEUR. A land-owning farmer.

- D -

DAMBALLA. An important voodoo god whose symbol is the serpent, and who is said to bring rain. The sacred color of this diety is white.

DAME-MARIE. Small coastal village on the western extremity of the southern peninsula.

DARTINGUENAVE, PHILIPPE SUDRE. First Haitian president elected under the U.S. occupation. He served from 1915 to 1922. He negotiated the treaty which legalized U.S. intervention in Haiti.
   Dartinguenave was a mulatto from the south of Haiti, the first southern mulatto to hold that office since 1879. He entered office committed to U.S. intervention, to the establishment of a U.S. customs receivership, and to the acceptance of a U.S. financial advisor, but he was determined not to surrender any control to the United States that he could avoid. Cooperation proved impossible when the U.S. forced an unacceptable treaty on Haiti. Dartinguenave had to walk a tight-rope between U.S. occupation authorities and the Haitian Assembly.

He was forced to capitulate to U.S. authorities on
many issues. He failed re-election in 1922.

DEBATMENT. According to voodoo belief, the struggle
between a person's soul and the gods which seek
to take possession of that person.

DE BEAUDIERRE, FERRAND. A grand blanc in Saint-
Dominique married to a mulatto, who in 1789 called
for the application of the French Declaration of the
Rights of Man to the mulattoes of the colony. He
was literally torn to bits by a white mob of fellow-
colonists.

DE LAS CASAS, BARTOLOME. Spanish priest who
sought to save the Indians of Hispaniola from ex-
tinction. One of his suggestions was to import
black slaves from Africa.

DE MARMELADE, COMTE. One of the leading noblemen
under the reign of King Henri Christophe in northern Haiti. His title derives from the area which
he governed.

DEPARTMENT (Departement). Unit of local government
of Haiti. The Constitution of 1957 and subsequent
legislation call for the internal division of the country into nine departments. The boundaries of these
departments are still to be determined. Mean-
while, the country is still divided into the five departments that existed in 1957; the departments of
the Artibonite, of the North, of the Northwest, of
the South, and of the West. See following entries.

DEPARTMENT OF THE ARTIBONITE. Political subdivision of Haiti corresponding generally to the lowland areas in the central part of the country. Its
principal cities are Saint Marc, Gonaïves, Verrettes,
Ennery, Montrouis, and Hinche.

DEPARTMENT OF THE NORTH. Political subdivision
in the northeastern portion of Haiti. Its principal
city is Cap-Haïtien. Other cities and towns of

importance are Le Borgne, Limbé, Fort-Liberté, Grande-Rivière-du-Nord, and Saint-Raphaël.

DEPARTMENT OF THE NORTHWEST. Political subdivision in the extreme northwestern part of Haiti. Its principal cities are Port-de-Paix, Môle-St.- Nicolas, and Baie-de-Henne.

DEPARTMENT OF THE SOUTH. Political subdivision of Haiti comprising the western two-thirds of the southern peninsula. Its principal cities are Jérémie, Les Cayes, Port Salut, Miragoâne, Petit- Trou-de-Nippes, Pestel, Dame-Marie, Anse-d'Hainault, Les Anglais, and Aquin.

DEPARTMENT OF THE WEST. Political sub-division in the southeastern (!) part of the country. Its principal city is the national capital, Port-au-Prince. Other cities and towns of importance are Léogane, Petit-Goâve, Pétionville, Jacmel, Marigot, Kenscoff, Trouin, Côtes-de-Fer, Bainet, Belle-Anse, Manneville, Mirebalais and Lafond.

DEPESTRE, RENE. Haitian poet whose works, Minerai Noir and Traduit du Grand Large, denounce the white world, express nostalgia for Africa and cry out for human brotherhood. He is said to be in exile in Cuba as of the 1970's.

DE PRADINES, EMERANTE. Organizer of Haitian folk dance troupes.

DERNIERE PRIERE. Literally, "last prayer," dedicated to a dead person and usually made nine days after a funeral.

DE RONCERAY, HUBERT. Director of the Haitian Center for Research in the Social Sciences, located in downtown Port-au-Prince.

DESINOR, CLOVIS M. Minister of Finance in Haiti in 1969. Désinor was born in St. Marc in 1914. He was a member of the Griots and Fignolé's Worker-

Farmer Movement. A civil servant, he served in
the ministries of health and interior, became secretary general of the president's office (under Magloire), and was assigned to the ministry of foreign
affairs and later became director of the national
economic planning bureau. He was considered a
possible successor to President François Duvalier
before the latter had his son designated to the office.

DESPARBES. French governor of Saint-Dominique in
1792 and 1793.

DESRENCE, LAMOUR. Leader of Haitian resistance
against France in the early 1800's.

DESSALINES, JEAN-JACQUES (1758-1806). An ex-slave
who became General-in-Chief in command of black
troops opposing French efforts to regain control of
Saint-Dominique (Haiti). Called "Father of the
Country," he was first made Governor-General for
Life, then, on September 22, 1804, was crowned
Emperor under the name of Jacques I. In November 1803, French forces in Saint-Dominique surrendered to General Jean-Jacques Dessalines. On
January 1, 1804, Dessalines proclaimed the Republic of Haiti, the first colony in Latin America to
sever its ties with the Old World.
    Dessalines attained his position as head of the
new Haitian nation by brute force and military
prowess. As the former slave of a freed Negro
(about the lowest level in French colonial society),
he received little education and he had no special
natural talent for civilian leadership.
    Dessalines established an economic system that
was akin to serfdom. All persons except soldiers
were "attached as cultivators to a plantation."
This system established the foundations for a Haitian peasantry.
    Historians have described Dessalines as an il-
literate who hated whites and persecuted mulattoes.
Indeed, in 1804, Dessalines issued an order for
the extermination of all French residents still in

Haiti. In a few weeks he had slaughtered the entire French population, men, women and children, except for a few priests and professional men.

Dissatisfaction with his stern discipline and repressive measures grew, and in 1806 he was ambushed and killed near Port-au-Prince. So violent were the feelings of his assassins that his body was horribly mutilated. The principal army barracks behind the Presidential Palace are named after Dessalines, and President François Duvalier is said to have modeled a good deal of his own conduct after this now popular Haitian hero.

DESTINE, JEAN LEON. Director of the government-sponsored Folklore Troupe of Haiti.

DEVOIT, CHARLES. A black commander who continued to resist French forces in Haiti even after the surrender of Toussaint L'Ouverture and Dessalines.

DIAQUOI, LOUIS. A leading Haitian poet and journalist who founded the group, Les Griots, in 1935.

DIMANCHE, ANDRE. One of Haiti's better known sculptors.

DJON-DJON. A mixture of black mushrooms and rice, sweetened by coconut.

D'OGERON, BERNARD. Governor of Tortuga beginning in 1665. D'Ogeron was able to control the buccaneers on the island and to develop small towns by importing women from France. By 1675, the year of his death, most of the buccaneers had become planters, and the western part of Hispaniola had become French, giving France a foothold on and claim to the area.

DOMINIQUE, MAX. Colonel in the Haitian Army, married to Marie Denise, sister of President Jean-Claude Duvalier. In 1967 President François Duvalier, believing that then Lt. Col. Dominique was plotting against him, exiled the young officer as

titular ambassador to Spain. A month later, he
was dismissed from the army and ordered to stand
trial for treason. The charges against him were
eventually dropped. He was reinstated in the army
and assigned as ambassador to France. In 1976,
he was living in voluntary exile in the United States.

DOMINIQUE, MICHEL. Commander-in-Chief of the Haitian Army, then President of Haiti from June 11,
1874, to April 15, 1876. Under his rule, a Treaty
of Amity, Commerce and Navigation was agreed
upon with the Dominican Republic which consider-
ably improved relations between the two countries.

DOMINIQUE, RAMEAU. The real ruler of Haiti from
1874 to 1876 under the presidency of his uncle,
Michel Dominique.

DORET, FREDERIC. Author of a series of booklets in
Creole, published under the general title, Biblio-
thèque Haïtien, designed as a collection for funda-
mental education in Haiti.

DORSAINVIL, J. C. A Haitian ethnologist who stressed
the literary value of Haitian folklore.

DOSSA (Dossu). The first female (male) child born after twins.

DOUGLASS, FREDERICK (ca. 1817-1895). A former U.S.
slave who became U. S. Ambassador to Haiti from
1889 to 1891. An admirer of the Haitian Revolution, he was placed in a dilemma when he was in-
structed by the U. S. Government to assist the U. S.
Navy in negotiations for a base at Môle-St. -Nicol-
as, which would be a threat to Haitian sovereignty
and independence.

DROGUE see ARRET

DUCHILLAU. French count and governor of Saint-Dominque until 1790. He sought to promote trade between the colony and the United States but was

successfully opposed by French merchants, who wished to maintain a commercial monopoly with Saint-Dominique.

DUFFAUT, PREFETE. One of Haiti's better known artists.

DUNCAN, PETER. Baltimore shipmaster who in 1857 took possession of the island of Navassa, 30 miles off the southern coast of Haiti, under terms of the U.S. Guano Islands Act of 1856, thus precipitating a crisis of ownership between the United States and Haiti.

DUPERIER, CHEVALIER. Grand blanc who was especially kind to his slaves. When the slave rebellion broke out, his slaves returned his kindness by giving him an armed escort to safety.

DUPERIER, ODILON. A Haitian artist known particularly for his carved masks.

DUPUY, BARON. An advisor to King Henri Christophe. Dupuy was a mulatto who served under Dessalines without acquiring any high position. He migrated to Philadelphia, where he became rich, and returned to Haiti when the reign of Christophe seemed to promise peace and tranquility. He was talented and well educated and became Christophe's secretary and interpreter and helped with practical administration of the Kingdom.

DURAND, OSWALD. 19th-century lyric poet who wrote in both French and Creole.

DURIAN. Fruit from Asia that has a bad smell but good taste and is eaten by many Haitians who believe it acts as an aphrodisiac.

DUVALIER, FRANÇOIS (1907-1971). A Haitian country doctor who took power in 1957 and ruled Haiti with an iron hand until his death in 1971. His nickname was Papa Doc.

Duvalier was born in 1907 a few blocks from
the National Palace during the military dictatorship
of Nord Alexis. He was the son of Duval Duvalier, a primary school teacher, and Uritia Abraham, a bakery worker. He attended primary and
secondary school at the Lycée Pétion in Port-au-
Prince and graduated from the medical school in
1934. He gained fame for his part in a campaign
to eliminate yaws and was named Director of Public Health, then Minister of Public Health and
Labor. He was elected president of the republic
on September 22, 1957, and later had himself designated President-for-Life. He was able to amend
the Constitution to permit him to name his successor and in early 1971, when his health was failing,
he was able to lower the age for President-for-
Life to 18 so as to be able to designate his 18-
year-old son, Jean-Claude, as the person to replace him. The transition took place a short time
later without undue disruption in the work of government.

François Duvalier was one of the cruelest and
most ruthless dictators of the 20th century.
Through a combination of techniques, including the
use of informers, secret police, voodoo and terror,
he suppressed all effective opposition to his regime.
He purged the army of disloyal or potentially disloyal elements and required the principal comman-
ders to report to him personally. The dreaded
"ton-ton macoutes" were appointed by him and owed
him personal loyalty. He gained control of the
press and exiled foreign Roman Catholic clergy.
In his later years, he became paranoic, suspecting
everyone, trusting no one, and taking the most
elaborate security precautions. Numerous attempts
were made to overthrow his regime, both by exiles
and malcontents within the country, but none succeeded and he died a natural death in 1971, after
14 years of tyranny.

Duvalier extolled the virtues of Africanism and
Negritude and succeeded in "blackening" the government during his years in power, that is, the re-
placing of whites and mulattoes with blacks. But

these were for the most part middle-level blacks
that he elevated to more influential positions. He
did little for the black masses of the country during his years in power.
   The most significant accomplishments of his
regime were the construction of an international
airport at Port-au-Prince, which bears his name,
and the Peligré Dam, near the Dominican border,
which provides water for irrigation and for the
generation of electric power. Otherwise his rule
is remembered for the suppression of liberty and
the brutal and naked application of power against
all enemies of the state, real or imagined.

DUVALIER, JEAN-CLAUDE. President-for-Life of Hai-
      ti. He took office in 1971 at the age of 19, the
      world's youngest president at that time. Heavy
      and rotund, he was a fair student and was consid-
      ered somewhat of a playboy. As president, he
      was under the strong influence of his mother dur-
      ing the first two years in office but began to as-
      sert his personal power beginning in 1974.

DUVALIER, MARIE DENISE. President Jean-Claude
      Duvalier's sister who was secretary to her father,
      François Duvalier, during his last years in office.
      She is married to Max Dominique, formerly an
      officer in the Palace Guard. She and her husband
      are now in exile in the United States.

DUVALIER, SIMONE OVIDE. Wife of François Duvalier
      and mother of Jean-Claude Duvalier, President-for-
      Life of Haiti. She is considered to wield consid-
      erable influence over her son.

- E -

ECONOMY. Haiti is proud that she effected the first
      extensive land reform in the Western Hemisphere.
      In the forty years following independence, the great
      sugar plantations were divided into small plots and
      distributed to soldiers and liberated slaves. Thus,

the hated symbol of oppression was destroyed. But
in the process, the base of the country's wealth
was destroyed. An efficient and productive sugar
economy was converted into a system of subsistence
farming.

Haiti has never recovered from the effects of
this 19th-century land distribution. Coffee was introduced as a crop requiring less labor and more
suited to small holdings. Finally, sugar was re-
introduced, but it never achieved the pre-eminence
of former years. Though a few large sugar and
sisal plantations do exist, most Haitian agriculture
today consists of tilling small holdings for the family table--rice, corn, beans and fruits and vegeta-
bles--with small surpluses being sold at the market or to exporters. Farming methods are primitive; the soil is exhausted and eroded; and there
is little cash for fertilizer.

Still, agriculture accounts for more than half
Haiti's gross national product and foreign exchange
earnings, mainly because other sectors with poten-
tial--mining, industry and tourism, for example--
remain relatively undeveloped. Haiti has a wide
variety of ores in several locations, but only copper and bauxite are mined, and in only two places.
Other areas are practically inaccessible.

There are 210 or more light industries in the
country, mostly transformation industries, where
components are imported for the purpose of taking
advantage of Haiti's cheap labor (about $2 per
day), and the assembled product is exported. This
involves mainly embroidered and decorated wearing
apparel and sporting goods. Almost all of the
baseballs used in the United States are stitched in
Haiti. The Government offers attractive incentives
to new industry--long-term tax exemptions, pro-
tection of the local market from foreign competition,
and import duty exemption on raw materials, building supplies and equipment.

Tourism has never developed its potential, mainly because of inadequate hotels and infrastructure.
Port-au-Prince docks can not accommodate tourist
ships. They must anchor at sea and transfer their

passengers to launches. Likewise, because of inadequate roads, it is difficult to reach the good
beaches or see the interior. Domestic air service
is inadequate. Still, Haiti remains a favorite tourist destination because of its lower prices, exotic
beauty, mystery, contrasts, primitive paintings
and astounding monuments, for example, the Citadel of King Henri Christophe and his Sans Souci
Palace near Cap-Haïtien.

The Government has begun to deepen and improve Port-au-Prince harbor facilities, and hotel
rooms under construction are expected to double
accommodations (from 700 to 1400 rooms). Yet
Haiti will probably not develop tourism to the level
of other Caribbean countries for some time because
of the time, money and energy necessary to over-
come the remaining infrastructural obstacles.

During the reign of the elder Duvalier, tourists
avoided Haiti because of fear of violence and police
state oppression. Under the son, the political cli-
mate has greatly improved. Haiti is now one of
the safest tourist destinations in the Caribbean.
Despite the poverty that abounds, one can safely
walk the streets of the capital at night or drive
through the countryside without fear. The Haitians
are basically a friendly people without hostility toward foreigners.

Until recently, the Haitian economy was hampered
by continual power stoppages, but this was over-
come in the early 1970's with the opening of a major hydro-electric plant in the Peligré Canyon near
the border of the Dominican Republic. The dam,
built at a cost of $30 million (and financed by the
Haitian Government!) is the world's highest and
holds back 328 million cubic meters of water,
which is used for irrigation as well as for the
generation of electricity.

Haiti's finances are currently in good condition.
The gourde is probably the world's most stable
currency in relation to the U.S. dollar. Five Haitian gourdes have equalled one U.S. dollar since
1919. The country has built up its foreign re-
serves and is servicing its debt on schedule. In-

come is mainly from tax receipts, and the principal expenditure is for the salaries of a 40,000-man
government bureaucracy.

Haitian exports consist mainly of coffee (about
50 percent), sugar (nearly all to the United States),
bauxite, sisal, handicrafts (Haiti supplies almost
all the mahogany products sold as souvenirs throughout the Caribbean), copper and light industrial products. Imports are principally from the United
States and include cotton textiles, wheat, machinery, petroleum products and electrical goods.

In the early 1960's, at the height of repression
by the first Duvalier regime, President Kennedy
broke off U.S. aid to Haiti, and most international lending agencies followed suit. However, under
the younger Duvalier, as a result of a change in
government attitudes, foreign aid has resumed.

ELIE, FREDERICK. An agent sent by Haitian President
Hyppolite to the United States in 1889. Admiral
Bancroft Cherardi of the U.S. Navy produced a
document purporting to be a copy of proposals made
by Elie to the U.S. Government offering the port,
Môle-St.-Nicolas, in return for U.S. aid. This
document was later proved to be nothing more than
an extract from a message prepared by U.S. Consul Stanislous Goutier.

ELIE, JUSTIN. Haitian composer, noted for his use of
Haitian folk rhythms, melodies and legends.

EMIGRES. Whites of Saint-Dominique whose property
was confiscated and who were exiled for acts against
the state.

EMPEROR JACQUES I   see   DESSALINES

ENFANTIN. Kindergarten. Primary school in Haiti is
usually preceded by two years of public kindergarten.

ENGAGE. A hired European hand in Haiti in the early
18th century.

ENGAGEMENT. According to voodoo belief, an agreement made with a voodoo god by which the latter
performs certain services in return for a fixed re-
ward.

ENNERY. Village in the north central part of Haiti.

ERZILIE (Erzulie). A Haitian voodoo goddess of considerable importance who is said to inhabit the water. She is regarded as a pale, trembling woman
of great wealth and ostentation.

ESPAÑOLA. Name given to the island now shared by
Haiti and the Dominican Republic upon its discovery
by Columbus in 1492. The term has been anglicized as "Hispaniola. " See also HISPANIOLA.

ESTIME, DUMARAIS (1900-1953). Black Haitian installed
as President in 1946. He purged the goverment of
mulatto officials and replaced them with blacks.
He discharged the debt to the United States and began a land reclamation project in the Artibonite
Valley. When in 1950 he attempted to amend the
Constitution to succeed himself, the army removed
him from office and sent him into exile.
Estimé was born in St. Marc in 1900. He studied law and became in turn a deputy from St. Marc,
President of the Chamber and finally President of
the Republic. He died in New York City in 1953.

ETANG SAUMATRE see LAKE SAUMATRE

EXCLUSIVE. Theory of the French economist, Jean
Baptiste Colbert, by which colonies should exist
only as a source of profit for France. Their products should not compete with French industry, and
they were allowed to trade only with France. As
might be expected, a rich contraband trade developed between Saint-Dominique and the United States
and England as a result of this restrictive commercial policy.

EXUME, RENE. One of Haiti's better known contemporary artists.

- F -

FAINE, JULES. Author of one of the first linguistic
    studies on Creole in Haiti entitled Philogie Creole
    and published in 1936.

FEINT. A sharp change in a folk dance step to avoid
    hypnotic effect of drums and gourds. Also called
    a "break."

FERMAGE. The practice of the government in seizing
    abandoned plantations and renting them to those who
    would make them productive. Half of the profits
    of the plantations belonged to the state while the
    other half was equally divided between proprietor
    and the workers. Working hours were regulated,
    and laborers were required to have government
    permission in order to leave the plantation. Fer-
    mage proved to be quite effective when properly
    enforced.

FERY, HONORE. First Minister of Public Education in
    Haiti in 1843. He encouraged the creation of rural
    schools financed by communities but subsidized by
    the government.

FIGNOLE, DANIEL. Mathematics teacher who turned
    politician in 1946 when he formed the Mouvement
    des Ouvriers et Paysans (Worker-Farmer Move-
    ment). He was an unsuccessful candidate in the
    Haitian election of 1957 and later worked in exile
    against the government of François Duvalier.
        Fignolé was one of the most effective orators of
    Haiti. He spoke in Creole and had the allegiance
    of nearly all the workers. But he lacked organi-
    zational skill and was unable to win over key ad-
    herents and delegate responsibility. He was pres-
    ident of Haiti for 19 days in 1957.

FIGUIER. Banyan or fig tree.

FIRMIN, JOSEPH-ANTENOR. Journalist, author, law-
    yer, cabinet minister, rebel and a Haitian exile in

St. Thomas, U. S. Virgin Islands.   In 1905, he published a book, M. Roosevelt, président des Etats-
Unis, et la République d'Haïti.   The theme of the
book is that Haiti had nothing to fear from the United States unless the Republic fell into anarchy, in
which case intervention might be welcome.   Haiti
could escape that experience through reform, he
said.

Firmin had formerly been Minister of Foreign
Affairs under President Hyppolite and successfully
fought off U. S. efforts to acquire a naval base at
Môle-St.-Nicolas.

Firmin believed that the executive power should
be the servant, not the master of the state, that
class divisions should be eliminated, and that the
rural masses of Haiti should be brought into Haitian society.

FORBES, CAMERON.   Chairman of a U. S. Commission
of Inquiry which investigated conditions in Haiti in
1930 under the U. S. occupation.   The commission
recommended reestablishment of the legislature and
and gradual return of public services to Haitian authority.

FORBES, GORDON.   British general who renewed the offensive against Saint-Dominique in 1796.   He was
defeated as a result of mulatto resistance and the
ravages of malaria and yellow fever.   He was replaced by British Lt. Gen. John Simcoe in 1797.

FORBES AND TUCKERMAN.   New York firm which unsuccessfully sought to settle 431 former U. S. slaves
on plantations at Ile-à-Vache off the southern coast
of Haiti in 1863 and 1864.   The black men were
mistreated and exploited.   The colony was abandoned at the insistence of the Haitian Government,
which seized the company's property to cover in-
debtedness.   This was the last attempt made to
settle U. S. freedmen in Haiti.

FORBES COMMISSION.   Commission appointed by President Herbert Hoover of the United States in 1930

with the task of making recommendations for termination of the U.S. occupation of Haiti.   The
Commission was composed of Cameron Forbes,
former U.S. Governor General of the Philippines;
Henry P. Fletcher, a career diplomat; Elie Vezina,
Secretary of L'Union St. Jean Baptiste d'Amérique;
and James Kerney and William Allen White, editors.

FOREIGN BONDHOLDERS PROTECTIVE COUNCIL.   A
    corporation formed in 1933 at the suggestion of the
    U.S. Government to look out for the interests of
    holders of Haitian Government bonds.

FORT.   Strong.   As a term related to voodoo, one who
    is especially adept at summoning and commanding
    the gods.

FORT DAUPHIN.   Scene of the massacre of 800 white
    planters and their families in 1794.   At the insti-
    gation of Jean François, then fighting with Spanish
    invaders, the blacks of this town, some 40 miles
    from Cap-François, fell upon the planters and
    slaughtered every one of them.

FORT DIMANCHE.   Prison near Port-au-Prince where
    "enemies" of the regime were incarcerated.

FORT LIBERTE.   Town in the northeastern corner of
    Haiti near the frontier with the Dominican Republic.

FOUCHE, FRANK.   Haitian dramatist of the early 20th
    century who, with F. Morisseau-Leroy, adapted
    the classical works, Oedipus Rex and Antigone,
    into Creole.

FRANÇOIS, JEAN.   Early slave leader who fled to the
    interior as a maroon.   He alternately waged war
    and peace against the French.   Toussaint L'Ou-
    verture first served under his command.   Both
    François and Toussaint joined the Spanish army as
    one way to fight the French.   François is respon-
    sible for inciting the massacre of some 800 white
    Frenchmen by their slaves in July 1794 at Fort

Dauphin near Cap-François. Toussaint later defected to the French, but François took refuge in
Spain.

FREEDMAN (Affranchi). Blacks and mulattoes who were
able to obtain their freedom in colonial Saint-Dominique. They formed the intermediary class between the colonists on the one hand and the slaves
on the other. The liberal professions were barred
to them, and they were forbidden from learning any
trade. They could not become Army officers, and
they were forced to wear clothes of material different from that worn by the whites.

FROMAGER. Kapok or cottonwood tree.

FURCY. A small village, beyond Pétionville and Kenscoff, at an elevation of 7000 feet. This area is
known as the "Haitian Alps."

- G -

GALBAUD. French Governor of Saint-Dominique in 1793.
He sided with the white planters and lost his power
in a test of strength with Sonthonax, the French
commissioner, who sided with the mulattoes and
blacks.

GAMELLE. A large wooden bowl used in preparing and
serving food.

GANGAN. Synonym for HOUNGAN.

GANGE. Black commander who continued to resist
French forces in Haiti even after the surrender of
Toussaint L'Ouverture and Dessalines.

GARCIA Y MORENO, CAPT.-GEN. JOAQUIN. Commander of the Spanish garrison at Santo Domingo in
colonial times. In 1793, he launched an invasion
of Saint-Dominique with 14,000 men. He gained
control of most of the North Province except for

Môle-St.-Nicolas, in the hands of the British, and
Cap-François and Port-de-Paix, in the hands of
the French. Several black rebels from Saint-Dominique served under his command, including Toussaint L'Ouverture. Later, when he had gained
control of Saint-Dominique, Toussaint and his brother, Paul, subdued Captain-General García and
conquered Santo Domingo.

GARDE see ARRET

GARDE D'HAITI see NATIONAL GUARD

GARDE PRESIDENTIEL. Palace guard established in
    1959 by President François Duvalier.

GAZETTE DE SAINT-DOMINIQUE. Haiti's first news-
    paper, a weekly established in the 18th century.

GEDE (Ghede). A voodoo god who is said to operate
    under the direction of Baron Samedi. He is con-
    sidered to be a zombie and is fed apart from other
    dieties. He is said to like clairin and to "eat" salt
    herring, hot peppers, cassava and roasted food.

GEFFARD, FABRE NICOLAS (1806-1878). Appointed
    President of Haiti on December 23, 1858, Geffard
    took the oath of office on January 20, 1859. He
    negotiated with the Holy See regarding the position
    of the Catholic Church in Haiti. The Pope wanted
    to send an Apostolic Prefect to Haiti and establish
    complete control of the church in that country.
    Geffard insisted on the right to participate in the
    appointment of bishops and archbishops.
        Geffard reorganized the Army and established
    new schools. But his strong rule provoked rebel-
    lion and he resigned in disgust and despair on
    March 13, 1867. He spent the remainder of his
    life in Jamaica, and died on December 31, 1878.

GENS DE COULEUR. Literally "persons of color."
    They were the free persons of African ancestry in
    French colonial Haiti. They were also known as

affranchis, or freedmen, and were mainly mulattoes, the result of unions between black slaves and
white masters.   They were permitted to own property and many were wealthy.   By 1791 they owned
a third of the land of Saint-Dominique and one-
fourth of the slaves.   They were often persons of
culture educated in France.

At first, being a small group, they enjoyed full
rights as French citizens.   Later, as they grew in
number and power, their rights were curtailed.
Generally speaking the gens de couleur resented the
grand blanc, detested the petit blanc and despised
the blacks, whom they considered their inferiors.

GEOGRAPHY.   Haiti is a small country, 10,700 square
miles in size, about the size of Albania or the
State of Maryland.   It occupies the western third
of the island of Hispaniola (the Dominican Republic
occupying the eastern two-thirds) and lies a scant
48 miles across the Windward Passage from Cuba.

Haiti is shaped like the open jaws of a dragon
about to devour a choice morsel (the island of Gonâve).   See map on page xvi.   In the language of
the native Indians, haiti meant highland, an apt
designation in view of the fact that three quarters
of the country consists of rough, mountainous ter-
rain, a higher proportion even than Switzerland.
Less than a quarter of the surface is cultivable.
However, it is a country rich in color and natural
beauty, with sweeping plains, azure seascapes and
flowering vegetation.

All parts of Haiti have a warm and even tem-
perature, with an annual mean of 66° F in the
mountains and about 81° at sea level.   The relative humidity is a bit high but quite tolerable,
ranging from 50° to 80° in the capital.

For administrative purposes, the country is divided into five départements: Department of the Artibonite in the central part; Department of the North
in the northeast corner; Department of the Northwest on the northwest peninsula; Department of the
South on the western two-thirds of the southern peninsula; and Department of the West in the southeast

corner.   See also DEPARTMENT.

GEORGES PLANTATION.   Scene of the betrayal of Toussaint L'Ouverture by French General Brunet in
1803.   The French general lured Toussaint to the
Georges Plantation near Gonaïves under the pre-
tense of discussing mutual problems.   He pledged
Toussaint's safety and security as an officer and
gentlemen of the French Army.   Once inside the
plantation, Toussaint was bound and hustled aboard
a French vessel, where he was shipped to France
and died a slow death in a French dungeon.

GERANT.   A farm manager in Haiti who lives and works
on someone else's land for a salary or the use of
part of the land.

GHERARDI, BANCROFT (1832-1903).   U. S. Admiral sent
to Port-au-Prince in 1891 with instructions to secure a lease on Môle-St.-Nicolas.   Admiral Gherardi employed many tactics, including pressure,
subterfuge and military threats to try to gain his
objective, but Haitian authorities protested, pro-
crastinated and successfully resisted the pressures.

GHUEVO.   A small chamber with an altar used for voodoo worship.

GILLES.   Early slave leader who was killed, beheaded
and exposed on the gallows for four days.

GONAIVES.   City on the Gulf of Gonâves, with a population of about 10,000.

GONAVE, GULF OF.   Immense bay separating the northwest and southwest regions of Haiti.

GONAVE, ISLAND OF.   Island in the Gulf of Gonâve at
the entrance of the harbor to Port-au-Prince.   It
is about 88 square miles and of rugged topography.
Its highest point, Morne la Pierre, rises to more
than 2500 feet.

GOURDE. Unit of Haitian currency. Five Haitian
     gourdes have equaled one U.S. dollar since 1919.
     The Haitian gourde is tied to the U.S. dollar by
     Haitian law and through agreement with the Inter-
     national Monetary Fund.

GOURGUE, ENGUERRAND. Contemporary Haitian art-
     ist, known especially for his lush baroque jungle
     scenes.

GOVERNMENT. Contemporary Haiti is a republic in
     form and a dictatorship in fact. The government
     is based on the Constitution of 1964, as amended.
     This constitution provides for strong executive au-
     thority vested in the president as chief of state and
     head of government. The legislature, called the
     Assembly, is unicameral with little power. Fifty-
     eight deputies are elected for six-year terms and
     are indefinitely re-eligible. The two principal ad-
     visory organs to the president are the Cabinet and
     the Great Technical Council of Natural Resources
     and Economic Development.
          The judiciary and the territorial organization
     are on the French pattern. The highest court is
     the Court of Cassation which has both appellate
     jurisdiction and the right of judicial review. The
     country is divided into départements which in turn
     are divided into arrondissements which in turn are
     divided into communes.
          The elder Duvalier did not permit political op-
     position. The only legal party under his rule was
     the National Unity Party. In 1959, 58 Duvalierists
     ran for the 58 Assembly seats without opposition.
     There has been liberalization under his son to the
     extent that 300 candidates--some independent--ac-
     tually contested for the 58 seats in 1973.
          Both father and son have followed a policy of
     "blackening" the government, that is, replacing
     whites and mulattoes with full-blooded blacks where-
     ever possible.

GOVI. A red earthen vessel in which, according to voo-
     doo belief, the spirits of the dead or of voodoo

gods are kept.   This term is not to be confused
with "canari," which refers to all earthen vessels.

GRAN (Grande).   In Creole, the meaning is "good".
(The Creole word for big or important is gros.)

GRANDE' ANSE.   Third largest river of Haiti, emptying
into the Gulf of Gonâve near the town of Jérémie.

GRANDE-RIVIERE-DU-NORD.   Village in the north-central part of Haiti.

GRANDE SALINE.   Salt ponds on the Artibonite delta
from which salt is made through the evaporation
process.

GRAN' MAIT'.   The Creole term for God as the ultimate
force in the universe.

GRAN' MOUN.   The Creole term for good or important
person, often a very old person, a grandfather or
a grandmother.

GREAT TECHNICAL COUNCIL OF NATURAL RESOURCES
AND ECONOMIC DEVELOPMENT.   A principal advisory group to the President of Haiti.

GRIFFON.   The descendant of a first-generation mulatto
and a pure-blood black.

GRILLOT.   Fried pork.

GRIS-GRIS.   A charm or talisman considered to have magic properties.

GROS-BON-ANGE.   The soul of a person.

GROS-BOUZAIN.   Dance characterized by a circular
grinding of the hips, usually performed during carnival and considered obscene by many French plantation owners who prohibited its performance.

GROS HABITANT (or Gros Neg).   Rural persons of

wealth and power. The gros habitant derives his status from large landholdings and leadership positions within the community. In spite of greater wealth, this group is identified with the peasants because they remain part of the rural masses rather than the urban class. Their status is regional. They wield little or no power at the national level. They may conduct a small business and have a larger house or more common-law wives. Politically, the gros habitant controls rural Haiti. Many become section chiefs and act as liaison with the central government.

GROTTE A MINGUET. A cavern near Cap-Haïtien which the early Indians of the area held sacred. According to their belief, the Sun and the Moon escaped from this cave and went on to shine in Heaven.

GROUILLERE. A mass dance characterized by erotic pelvic movement.

GUACANAGARIC. Indian chief in the northwestern portion of Hispaniola who welcomed Columbus on his arrival in 1492. In return, Columbus' men ravished his domain.

GUANO. The droppings of birds, which are processed as fertilizer.

GUARIONEX. Indian chief of the Kingdom of Le Magna in the northeastern portion of Hispaniola in the early 16th century.

GUERRIER, GENERAL PHILIPPE (1757-1845). President of Haiti on May 3, 1844, at the age of 87. He died in office on April 15, 1845.

GUINGAND, NOEL. Black commander who continued to resist French forces in Haiti even after the surrender of Toussaint L'Ouverture and Dessalines.

- H -

HABITANT. A land-owning farmer in Haiti. A gros
     habitant is an important land-owning farmer.

HABITANT D'HAYTI. Anonymous author of a collection
     of poems in Creole, which is the first known ex-
     ample of a book in that language. It was published
     in Philadelphia in 1811 and reproduced in a booklet
     entitled, Gombo Comes to Philadelphia, by E. L.
     Tinker, in 1957.

HABITATION. In colonial times, a plantation. Even
     today, the usual way of describing a piece of land
     in Haiti is by the name of the plantation (or former
     plantation) on which it is located: HABITATION LE
     CLERC (see next entry) is example.

HABITATION LE CLERC. A multi-million dollar hotel-
     apartment complex high on a hillside overlooking
     Port-au-Prince, centered about the historic palace
     built in 1801 for General Charles Victor Le Clerc
     and his wife, Pauline. Forty-four apartment units
     are strung out at one-story level over a vast
     wooded acreage. It was designed by the Haitian
     architect, Albert Mangones.

HAITI, REPUBLIC OF. Nation occupying the western
     portion of the island of Hispaniola in the Caribbean
     Sea. The world's first black republic and the first
     nation in the Western Hemisphere (after the United
     States) to achieve its independence (1804), Haiti has
     an area of 10,700 square miles and a population
     estimated from 3.5 to 5.1 million. In the language
     of the native Indians, haiti meant "highland."

HAITIAN-AMERICAN DEVELOPMENT CORPORATION.
     U.S. investment company which leased public land
     in Haiti for the production of sisal. It also exper-
     imented with limited success with the cultivation
     of cryptostegia, a latex-producing vine.

HAITIAN CENTER FOR RESEARCH IN THE SOCIAL
SCIENCES. A private educational facility located
in Port-au-Prince. The center holds seminars and
conducts basic research in the social sciences.

HAITIAN CORPORATION OF AMERICA. U.S. investment
company which at one time owned the Plaine du
Cul-de-Sac Railroad, together with the Port-au-
Prince wharf, an electric plant, a tramway and
sugar plantations in Haiti. Its assets as of 1930
were about $11 million and it gave work to over a
thousand Haitians.

HALAOU. A black chief who, in order to preserve influence over his followers, pretended to be in communication with Heaven through a white cock, which
was his inseparable companion.

HAUT CHANT. Song of salutation to an important person or voodoo god.

HAYTI. Early spelling of "Haiti."

HAYTIAN REPUBLIC. American commercial vessel
which sailed from New York in 1889 on a regular
voyage to Haitian ports. It was held up by the
Government of President Légitime and accused of
having transported rebel troops and supplies. The
vessel was released when the United States sent
two warships to Port-au-Prince.

HEADS OF REGULATIONS. An Anglo-American state-
ment negotiated by Toussaint L'Ouverture in 1799
as part of a commercial treaty with the United
States, in which both the United States and Saint-
Dominique opposed the indoctrination of slaves of
either nation with "dangerous principles."

HEDOUVILLE, THEODORE. French special agent to
Haiti in 1798. He tried without success to rees-
tablish the authority of France in Saint-Dominique.
Hédouville tried to interest Toussaint and Rigaud
in leading an invasion of Jamaica. In October

1798, he left Saint-Dominique for France under
military pressure from Toussaint.

HENRI.   An Indian of Bahoruco who survived the massacre of Anacaona's followers in 1504.   He grew
up as a slave in Santo Domingo, but incensed by
the ill treatment inflicted upon him, he fled in
1519 with a few other Indian slaves similarly hu-
miliated by their masters.   They were joined by
black slaves and for 14 years fought off all efforts
to subdue them.   Charles V, then King of Spain,
sent a special agent to Hispaniola to make peace
with Henri.   A solemn treaty of peace was made
in 1533 by which Henri was allowed to reside in
the village of Boya with his 4000 followers.   He
was exempted from tribute and was henceforth
known as the "Cacique of Haiti. "

HERARD, CHARLES AINE (RIVIERE) (1787-1850).   A
simple soldier who lead an insurrection against
President Boyer on January 27, 1843.   He was
elected President on December 30, 1843, but he
lacked the qualities to make the transition from
military to civilian rule.   He alienated the inhabitants of the Spanish portion of the island, which
was lost in rebellion in 1844.   He sought to rule by
the sword and thus incurred distrust of the liberals
who had fashioned the Constitution of 1843.   He
fled to Jamaica on June 2, 1844.

HIGUEY.   Indian Kingdom in eastern Hispaniola under
the command of the chief, Cotubana.   Now a town
by that name in the same location.

HINCHE.   Village in the west-central portion of Haiti
about 30 miles from the border with the Dominican
Republic.

HISPANIOLA.   Island lying between Cuba and Puerto
Rico.   Haiti occupies the western third of the island, with the Dominican Republic occupying the
eastern two-thirds.   Discovered by Columbus on
his first voyage to the New World, on December

5, 1492. He took possession in the name of the
King of Spain, calling the island "La Isla Española," which was later anglicized to "Hispaniola."

For a short time Hispaniola flourished as the
center of all Spanish colonial activity, but the discovery of gold and silver on the American contin-
ent led to the virtual abandonment of the colony
by the Spanish.

HISTORY. Haiti's past is filled with turbulence and
bloodshed. In no other place has man's inhumanity
to man been greater over a longer period of time
than in this little corner of the world.

The coast of present-day Haiti was sighted by
Christopher Columbus on his first voyage to Amer-
ica on December 5, 1942. He took possession in
the name of the King of Spain, calling the island,
"La Isla Española," which later was anglicized to
"Hispaniola," its present name.

In December 1492, Columbus established the
first settlement in the New World at La Navidad,
between the present-day Haitian cities of Cap-Haïtien and Fort Liberté. When he returned on his
second voyage nearly a year later, he found that
the Indians had massacred the small garrison in
reprisal for the brutalities the settlers had inflicted
upon them.

It is estimated that there was close to a million
friendly Arawak Indians on the island of Hispaniola
when Columbus arrived. Within a few years, these
were completely decimated by the Spaniards, who
enslaved them, forced them to search for gold and
killed them off as inferior beasts.

Sugarcane was introduced, and blacks were imported from Africa to replace the near-extinct Ara-
waks. But Hispaniola never prospered under the
Spaniards. Only small quantities of gold and other
precious metals were found. The island became a
springboard for sallies further to the west (Peru
and Mexico, for example) when it was learned that
rich mines had been discovered there by Cortés
and Pizarro. The number of Spaniards at any one
time was never large, and commerce with Spain

was limited almost exclusively to sugar and hides.

French influence came in 1625 when buccaneers, preying on Spanish commerce in the Caribbean, established themselves on the tiny island of La Tortue (Tortuga) off the northwest coast. Subsequently they occupied the western part of Hispaniola. Spain, weakened in Europe, was in no position to resist, and the area now known as Haiti was ceded by Spain to France in 1697.

In the 18th century, under the control of France, Saint-Dominique, as the French called their new possession, became one of the richest colonies of the New World. Arts and letters developed, second only to the cultural centers of Europe. But this prosperity was exacted at the price of tremendous human sacrifice. Slaves were brought from Africa and worked under conditions so hard as to require constant replacement. Toward the end of the century, it was estimated that nearly half a million slaves were being supervised by some 60,000 whites and freedmen, an average of about eight slaves to every master.

The situation was ripe for explosion, and the spark came on the winds of the French Revolution, with its ideas of Liberty, Equality and Fraternity.

In 1790, the French National Assembly permitted the colonies to submit plans for self-government. The white colonists of Saint-Dominique were intent on denying participation to freedmen and mulattoes and also on preserving the institution of slavery. French-educated mulattoes who had been exposed to Jacobin thought led the first insurrection, but were easily crushed. Nevertheless, the incident incited further discontent among freedmen, who forced the colonists to agree in advance to any legislation the French National Assembly might make with regard to their status.

It was obvious to the Negro slaves that the mulattoes and freedmen were concerned only with their own fate and not with that of the slaves. So the slaves acted on their own behalf. To the beat of voodoo drums, they devastated the plantations and murdered their white owners. In a desperate effort

to prevent further bloodshed, French commissioners announced the abolition of slavery, but this
only served to anger the white planters and rein-
force the zeal of the rebels.

The French planters appealed to the British for
help, since at that time the British and French
were at war.   The British responded in the hope
of securing control of one of France's prized pos-
sessions.   This led to a five-year occupation by
the British.   During this period the French Government proclaimed the end of slavery in all French
colonies in an effort to stimulate rebellion against
the British.

This tactic proved successful in Saint-Dominique
as Toussaint L'Ouverture, a former slave who rose
to the rank of general in the Spanish Army in Santo Domingo, returned to his native land and led a
slave rebellion which forced the British to evacuate.   Toussaint not only took control of Saint-Dominique but of Santo Domingo as well.

The situation had also changed in France.   Napoleon had come to power with a pledge to restore
France's prestige.   He dispatched a fleet to Haiti,
took Toussaint prisoner to France (where he died
in chains), and sought to reinstitute slavery.   The
Haitians rose as one and, with the aid of a fortu-
itous yellow fever epidemic, which took thousands
of French lives, and belated assistance from the
British, finally gained independence in 1804, the
first Negro republic in the world and the first nation in the Western Hemisphere, after the United
States, to become free.

But Haiti was a ravaged nation, whose economic
base had been destroyed, whose white population
had been killed or had fled, whose remaining population was almost completely illiterate and inex-
perienced in self-government, and whose society
was riven with internal class dissension.   For over
a century, anarchy ruled and Haiti was isolated
from the world.

Finally, in 1915, fearful of French or German
intervention to collect debts owed them by Haiti,
the United States intervened.   The U.S. occupation

lasted until 1934 and was instrumental in helping
to modernize the country and in balancing revenues.
The U.S. withdrawal was followed by another
period of instability until François Duvalier, a
country doctor, took power in 1957. He ruled with
an iron hand until his death in 1971. He was succeeded by his son, Jean-Claude, who, like his father, bears the constitutional title of President-
for-Life.

HOLLY, THEODORE. Born in Washington, D.C., in
1829 of Catholic Negro parents, Theodore Holly
became bishop of Haiti in 1874 and died there in
1911.

HORSE. According to voodoo belief, a person who has
been "mounted" or possessed by his loa.

HOUNCI CANZO. According to voodoo belief, a person
who has gone through the second stage of voodoo,
whose loa has been "tamed" and who is therefore
in a position to assist in voodoo ceremonies.

HOUNFORT. Voodoo temple.

HOUNGAN. Voodoo priest. There are no assignments
of voodoo priests. Each becomes established in
an area as a result of his proven effectiveness as
a healer and diviner.

HOUNGENICON. Male who assists male voodoo priests
during voodoo ceremonies.

HOUNGFOR. Voodoo temple.

HUNSI. One of the first degrees of voodoo. The hunsi
know the rituals of voodoo in a general way, hold
and wave banners which honor the voodoo gods,
sing songs and otherwise assist the houngan.

HUNSI KANZO. A hunsi who has successfully passed
the ordeal by fire.

HUNTOR.   The spirit of the voodoo drum.   Also, the
voodoo spirit which may possess the drummer.

HYPPOLITE, FLORVILLE.   President of Haiti from October 9, 1889, to March 24, 1896.   He is remembered for his many public works.   A dark-skinned
member of the elite, he built bridges, introduced
the telegraph and the telephone to Haiti, and constructed new market places.   Under his leadership,
the government began to indulge in extravagances,
however, which led to uprisings in the South.   Hyppolite died in 1896 while leading an effort to quash
one such rebellion.

HYPPOLITE, HECTOR.   One of the more famous of the
Haitian primitive artists, born 1894.   He was a
voodoo priest who painted, often with a house-paint-
ing brush in bold strokes of bright color.   He died
of a heart attack in 1948 while painting his own
portrait.

- I -

IBO.   In Haiti, the name given to a group of voodoo gods.

IBO BEACH.   Small resort on Cacique Island, about an
hour's drive from Port-au-Prince, along the St.
Marc road.

ILE-A-VACHE.   Island off the Southern coast of Haiti.
In 1862, President Abraham Lincoln signed a contract with an adventurer, Bernard Kock, to settle
5000 freed U.S. slaves on the Ile-à-Vache.   About
431 were actually sent to the island in 1863 but
were removed within a year because of illness and
neglect.

ILE DE LA TORTUE   see   Turtle Island

INSTALLE.   Possessed by a voodoo god, who "installs"
himself in a person.

INSTITUTE OF AGRICULTURAL AND INDUSTRIAL DE-
VELOPMENT. Haiti's development bank.

INTERMEDIARY COMMITTEE (Commission Intermediare).
Group of six blacks and six whites that replaced
the colonial assembly in Haiti in 1792. For the
first time, representatives of the black race sat
in a political body in Haiti.

INTERNATIONAL ROUTE. A highway which parallels
the course of the Libon River and forms part of
the international boundary between Haiti and the
Dominican Republic.

- J -

JACQUES I. see DESSALINES

JACMEL. City of about 10,000 population in southern
Haiti.

JAEGERHUBER, WERNER. Collector, arranger and
publisher of Haitian folksongs and dances. He in-
corporated folksongs into an impressive operatic
arrangement of Romain's novel, "Masters of the
Dew. "

JEAN-FRANÇOIS. Leader of the slave rebellion of 1791.

JEREMIE. City on the southern peninsula of Haiti with
a population of about 10,000.

JOANTY, OCCIDE. Haitian composer known for his use
of Haitian folk rhythms, melodies and legends.

JOLICOEUR, AUBELIN. Journalist and former head of
Haiti's National Office of Tourism. Jolicoeur is
one of Haiti's most colorful personalities. Impec-
cably dressed in a white suit, with cane, he was
usually seen at the airport at the time of incoming
flights and became known as Haiti's unofficial

"greeter" until his appointment as minister of tourism by President-for-Life Jean-Claude Duvalier.

JOSEPH, ANTONIO.   Contemporary Haitian artist of considerable reknown.

JOSEPH, JASMIN.   Haitian artist, known particularly for his terracotta sculptures.

JUSTICE OF THE PEACE.   Lowest judicial unit in Haiti.   The justice of the peace operates at the level of the commune and has jurisdiction over all sections which compose the commune.

- K -

KANZO.   Ordeal by fire, as a rite of voodoo.

KENAF.   An hibiscus plant widely cultivated in Haiti for its fiber.

KENSCOFF.   Picturesque village in the mountains above Port-au-Prince.

KOCK, BERNARD.   An adventurer from New Orleans who persuaded Abraham Lincoln to sign a contract (1862) with him to settle 5000 freed U.S. slaves on the Ile-à-Vache, off the coast of Haiti, for $250,000.   The contract was repudiated when it was learned that Kock's reputation was shady.   A federal marshall in New York accused Kock of being a rebel who planned to take Lincoln's money and then sell his shipment into slavery.   His rights were bought out by the New York firm of Forbes and Tuckerman who shipped 431 colonists to the island in 1863.   Kock turned up as Project Director.   He collected the colonists' money on the pretext of converting it to Haitian currency and his own private scrip, but returned no money to them, refused to pay them wages and to provide adequate food, shelter or medical care.   On March 5, 1864, the surviving colonists returned to the United States on a U.S. transport.

KOKLO.   Creole term for chicken.

- L -

LA BROCHETTE GROUP.   A group of Haitian artists
   led by Luckner Lazare, who studied in Paris and
   sought to establish a contemporary style of national Haitian art.

LAFOND.   Village in the central part of Haiti on the
   Artibonite River.

LAFONTANE, DANIEL.   One of Haiti's better known
   contemporary artists.

LAFONTANT, EMILE.   One of Haiti's better known contemporary artists.

LAFORESTERIS, LOUIS EDMOND.   Early Haitian sculptor.

LAFORTUNE.   Black commander who continued to resist
   French forces in Haiti even after the surrender of
   Toussaint L'Ouverture and Dessalines.

LAKE PELIGRE.   Reservoir formed by the dam on the
   upper Artibonite River at the point of the conver-
   gence of the Montagnes Noir and the Chaîne de
   Mateaux.

LAKE SAUMATRE (Etang Saumâtre).   The largest of Haiti's lakes (70 square miles), it is a body of brack-
   ish water in the Cul-de-Sac close to the Dominican
   frontier.   It is a habitat of many species of exotic
   tropical wildlife.

LALEAU, LEON.   Haitian writer who deplored the U.S.
   occupation and discrimination against mulattoes in
   the book, Le Choc (The Shock), published in 1932.

LALWADI (also, Lalawaldi, La loi di or Lalawaldt).
   Literally, "the law says," it is a Creole term for
   a dance leader during carnival.

LA MAGUA.   Indian Kingdom in the northeast of Hispaniola, an area later called Vega Real.

LAMARTINIERE.   Black rebel commander at Crête-à-Pierrot who successfully resisted repeated attacks by LeClerc's forces.   When he could no longer resist, he successfully broke through French lines with his small garrison.

LAMBI.   Musical instrument made from the conch shell. It was used as a call to assembly and as a means of communication between slaves during the Haitian revolution.

LAMOTHE, LUDOVIC.   Haitian composer known for his use of Haitian folk rhythms, melodies and legends.

LA NAVIDAD.   First European settlement in the New World, established in 1492 by Columbus on the northern coast of present-day Haiti, between the present-day cities of Cap-Haïtien and Fort Liberté. When he returned a year later, Columbus found that the Indians had massacred the entire garrison. Columbus had left about 40 men with instructions to avoid trouble with the Indians, to seek gold and to explore the island.   The settlers treated the Indians ruthlessly and as a result, were exterminated.

LANGAGE.   Language spoken by voodoo priests during voodoo ceremonies.   It is of African origin and is assumed to be understood only by the gods and those inculcated into the voodoo faith.

LANGUAGE.   The official and commercial language of the country, and the language of the schools, is French.   However, French is spoken by only a small, educated elite, perhaps 10 percent of the population.   Peasants, who comprise the rest of the population, speak no French.   They speak Creole, a mixture of 16th- and 17th-century Norman French, the native Indian language, some Spanish, and Portuguese and African expressions and the simple syntax of English privateers.   The influ-

ence of the French language is strong in Haiti in
the legal and judicial system, in commerce and
culture and throughout the educational system.

LA PLACE.   The chief assistant and second-in-command
to the voodoo priest.   He is responsible for operating the temple during the priest's absence.

LARES.   Minor household dieties, according to the voodoo cult.

LA REVUE INDIGENE.   Literary journal founded in 1927
by a group of educated young Haitians curious about
Haitian voodoo and folkways.

LA RONDE.   Literary journal established in 1898 by
Massillon Coicou and other members of the literary
club, Les Emulateurs.

LA SELLE.   Highest peak in Haiti (8889 feet).

LA TORTUE   see   TURTLE ISLAND

LA TORTUGA   see   TURTLE ISLAND

LAURENT, CASIMIR.   One of Haiti's better known artists.

LAVEAUX, ETIENNE.   French field commander under
French commissioner Sonthonax and subsequently
governor-general.   He was rescued from a mulatto
attack by Toussaint L'Ouverture in 1796.   Laveaux
rewarded Toussaint by appointing him lieutenant
general.   From that moment on, he became a pup-
pet of Toussaint.

LAVE-TETE.   Literally, a "head wash," it is the first
stage in a voodoo initiation.   In this ceremony, the
"candidate" is cleansed of all impurities and is
"entered" by a voodoo god or goddess.

LAZARE, ADRIAN.   A U.S. citizen who contracted with
the Government of Haiti to establish a national bank

at Port-au-Prince. The Government agreed to provide $500,000 in capital, and Lazare was to put
up $1 million. When the necessary funds could not
be raised, the Government canceled the agreement.
Lazare then sued for breach of contract, and the
issue embittered relations between Haiti and the
United States for many years.

LAZARE, LUCKNER. Paris-trained Haitian artist who
sought beginning in the 20's to establish a new
contemporary style of national Haitian art.

LEAGUE FOR SOCIAL ACTION. A civic organization
formed in Haiti in 1929 to prevent a third term for
Haitian presidents, to bring about the restoration
of the functions of the legislature, and to end the
U. S. occupation.

LE BORGNE. Small town on the northern coast of Haiti.

LE CHOC (THE SHOCK). A book by Leon Laleau published in 1932, which criticizes the U. S. occupation and deplores discrimination against mulattoes.

LE CLERC, FRANÇOIS. A French pirate who destroyed
the small town of Yaguana (which was later rebuilt
as Port-au-Prince) in the year 1553.

LE CLERC, GENERAL CHARLES VICTOR EMMANUEL
(1772-1802). The brother-in-law of Napoleon Bon-
aparte who headed an expedition of 45,000 of the
best soldiers of France in an unsuccessful effort
to regain control of the colony of Saint-Dominique
for France. He died of yellow fever in Cap-Haïtien in 1802.
    Le Clerc's orders were explicit. He was first
to occupy the coastal towns. During this period,
the black generals were to be won over by flattery
and promotions. In the second phase, all resistance on the island was to be eliminated. If the
Haitian generals had not by then surrendered, they
were to be captured and executed. In the third
period, the blacks were to be put to work once
more.

The plan started off well for the French. Le Clerc's forces took possession of most of the island. The black generals, Henri Christophe, Toussaint L'Ouverture and Jean-Jacques Dessalines, made peace. But then yellow fever broke out on the island in epidemic proportions. The blacks were immune, but Le Clerc's forces were decimated. Le Clerc however tricked Toussaint into captivity and sent him off to France.

What made matters even worse was Napoleon's restoration of slavery on Guadeloupe. When this news reached the blacks of Saint-Dominique, they were sure that Le Clerc planned the same fate for them and resumed the struggle against Le Clerc with unmatched fervor, preferring death to captivity. Le Clerc pleaded for reinforcements, which he received, but the depletion of his forces by yellow fever continued. Le Clerc himself succumbed on November 2, 1802. The blacks resumed the offensive and Christophe and Dessalines returned to head the black insurgents. Within a year the French were driven from the island.

LECONTE, CINCINNATUS. President of Haiti from August 14, 1911, to August 8, 1912. He was killed on the latter date by an explosion in the presidential palace.

LEGBA. According to voodoo belief, the god which guards entrance ways. He is perceived as a limping old man in tattered clothes.

LEGITIME, FRANÇOIS DENYS (1842-1935). President of Haiti from December 16, 1888, to August 22, 1889. During this entire period, he was engaged in a fierce but ultimately losing struggle with General Florville Hyppolite for the office.

Légitime considered himself a champion of republican government against military autocracy but was unwilling to submit to the popular will. He was part of the educated mulatto elite who felt the need to "save" Haiti from a dictatorship founded upon the popularity of the black masses.

LE HEROS. The French warship which sped Toussaint
L'Ouverture from Saint-Dominique to France in
1802, following Toussaint's arrest by the French.

LE JEUNE CASE. A famous test case of the Black Code
in Saint-Dominique. Fourteen slaves protested to
the procuror-general of Cap Français the torture
of two black women suspected of poisoning slaves
in a work gang. An investigation confirmed the
torture, but because of white pressure, it was impossible to obtain a conviction of the slave master,
Le Jeune.

LE JEUNE HAITI. Magazine founded in 1894 by Justin
Lhérisson and other young intellectuals who had
been graduated from Lycée Pétion in Port-au-
Prince. The magazine was noted for its portrayal
of Haitian family life.

LE MARIEN. Kingdom in the northern part of Hispaniola under the command of the Indian chief, Guacanagaric, with its capital near present-day Cap-
Haïtien.

LEOGANE. City in Haiti west of Port-au-Prince.

LEONTUS, ADAM. Contemporary Haitian artist of considerable renown.

LEOPARDS. An elite unit of the Haitian army, answer-
ing directly to the minister of national defense.

LES ANGLAIS. Small town on the southern shore of the
southern peninsula.

LES CAYEMITES. Islands off the northern shore of
Haiti's southern peninsula.

LES CAYES. Principal town of the South Province of
Haiti, with a population of about 10,000.

LESCOT, ELIE (1883-   ). President of Haiti from 1941
to 1946. He was very pro-American. Shortly

after the Japanese attack on Pearl Harbor, Lescot declared war on Japan, Germany, Italy, Hungary, Bulgaria and Rumania. He took advantage of the war to convert himself into a virtual dictator. His government was brought down by revolution in 1946.

LESCOTITE. The name given to Haitian bauxite in honor of the Haitian President, Elie Lescot, who granted Reynolds Mining Company the first concession contract and facilitated the company's exploratory work.

LES EMULATEURS. Literary club in Haiti founded toward the end of the 19th century. Its members established a new literary journal, La Ronde.

LES GRIOTS. A Haitian group of the 1930's which emphasized négritude (blackness). Also, the name of the publication issued by this group. François Duvalier was one of its early members.

LETTRE DE DEMANDE. A written marriage proposal, usually delivered to the family of the girl by the oldest male in the suitor's family.

LHERISSON, JUSTIN. Founder in 1894 of the magazine, Le Jeune Haiti, famed for its portrayal of Haitian family life.

LIATAUD, GEORGES. Haitian artist, known particularly for his work with sheet iron.

LIBON RIVER. A stream near the border of Haiti and the Dominican Republic, which for many years served as a boundary between the two countries.

LIGUE POUR LE MAINTIEN DE L'INDEPENDENCE NATIONALE (LEAGUE FOR THE MAINTENANCE OF NATIONAL INDEPENDENCE). Propaganda agency set up to spread the idea that Florville-Hyppolite owed his success solely to aid rendered to him by the United States in exchange for a promise to cede the harbor of Môle-St.-Nicolas to the United States as a naval base and coaling station.

LIMBE.   Village in the north-central portion of Haiti.

LIMONADE, COMTE DE.   The title of the mulatto, Julian Prévost, who derived this title from the area of the North Province of Haiti which had been assigned to him to govern.   An intelligent young man educated in France, he was designated Secretary of State and Minister of Foreign Affairs in the Kingdom of Henri Christophe.   He published an account of Christophe's rise to the monarchy entitled, Rélation des glorieux événements qui ont porté leurs Majestés Royales sur le train d'Hayti; suivi de l'histoire du couronnement et du sacre du Roy Henry Ier, et de la Reine Marie-Louise (Cap Henry, 1811).   He was one of the most capable of Christophe's advisors.

LOA.   Voodoo god which, according to the voodoo faith, is capable of "possessing" a voodoo worshiper.   After a person is "mounted" by a loa, he is treated with deference and respect by other members of the community.   According to voodoo belief, a loa may occupy only the head or the entire body of his subject.   Worshipping the loa is the chief means of perpetuating the voodoo cult.

LOA ACHETE.   A voodoo god that can be purchased.

LOA NAN CANARIE.   According to voodoo belief, a loa taken from the depths of a stream and kept in a jar.

LOA TRAVAIL.   Voodoo dieties with great capacity for work.

LOUP GAROU.   A werewolf, half man, half wolf.

L'OUVERTURE, PAUL.   Brother of Toussaint.   He conducted a successful expedition against Santo Domingo but surrendered the garrison in error to the French.   He remained for some time in the service

of France in Saint-Dominique but was later executed by a desperate and fearful Rochambeau.

L'OUVERTURE, TOUSSAINT see TOUSSAINT L'OU-
    VERTURE

LÜDERS, EMIL. A German citizen who the German
    Kaiser believed had been wrongly imprisoned in
    Haiti in 1897. The Germans demanded the release
    of Lüders, the removal of the judge involved, the
    imprisonment of police officers involved, and the
    payment of a $5000 indemnity for each day the man
    had spent in jail. Haitian President Simon Sam
    agreed to the release of Lüders, offered to arbi-
    trate other claims, and appealed to the United
    States to enforce the Monroe Doctrine against Ger-
    many. President McKinley would only agree to
    help mediate the dispute. German cruisers ap-
    peared on the scene and President Sam was given
    three hours to decide whether he would pay an in-
    demnity of $20,000 or face a bombardment. He
    chose to pay.

LUTIN. According to voodoo belief, ghosts of young
    children who have died before being baptized.

LYCEE PETION. Haiti's first high school, started in
    the 19th century by Alexander Pétion.

                      - M -

MACANDAL, FRANÇOIS. A fugitive slave who organ-
    ized a plot to poison whites. He was burned
    at the stake in 1758. Macandal had come from
    Guinea. He escaped to the hills and became
    a maroon (fugitive slave). A gifted orator, he
    persuaded his followers that he was immortal.
    He pillaged the plantations but at the same
    time left behind an organization of followers.
    He plotted to poison the water in every house
    in the capital of the province on a certain day
    and to fall on the whites while they were   in

convulsions and dying. His boldness was his down-
fall. He went to a plantation, got drunk, was be-
trayed, captured and burned alive.

MACKANDAL, FRANÇOIS see MACANDAL

MACOUTE. A straw bag carried by peasants.

MADA SARA (Madâm Sara). Term applied to female
itinerant traders. Originally the term applied to
a migratory bird which flies from place to place
searching for food. Such traveling sales ladies
are a critical link in the Haitian marketing system.

MAGISTRATE COMMUNAL. Chairman of a communal
council and thus, in effect, "mayor" of a city or
town.

MAGLOIRE, PAUL EUGENE (1907-). A black leader
and army colonel who succeeded to the presidency
of Haiti in 1950. He was accused of despotic rule
and corruption and overthrown in 1956. His regime is remembered for having insituted economic
planning, attempting to attract industries to Haiti,
securing U.S. aid, improving the nation's infrastructure and encouraging tourism.

MAINGUY, SIEUR. Slave owner who was convicted of
torturing his slaves. He was fined 10,000 livres
and prohibited from ever owning slaves again.

MAIT. Master, as in Gran' Maît' (God) or Maît Tête
(the loa that has possessed a person).

MAIT CARREFOUR. The voodoo god of the crossroads
who commands the traffic through them.

MAITLAND, GENERAL THOMAS. Last commander of
the British expedition against Saint-Dominique. In
1798, he signed a secret agreement with Toussaint
L'Ouverture, ending five years of British occupation.

MAIT' TETE.   According to voodoo belief, a spirit which
    has entered and possessed a person's mind.

MAJOR-DOMO.   Leader of a carnival or Easter group
    of dancers.

MALANGAN.   A type of yam.

MAMALOI.   Term used in popular literature to desig-
    nate a priestess of the voodoo cult.   A more pre-
    cise term is mambo or mambu.

MAMAN.   Mother; also, the largest of the trio of voodoo
    drums.

MAMBO (Mambu).   Priestess of voodoo.

MAMEY (Mammee).   A common fruit in Haiti which is
    eaten raw, made into preserves or fed to livestock.

MANA.   According to voodoo belief, the power lying
    within a holy object.

MANCHETTE.   A long utility knife used by Haitian peas-
    ants and workers in various agricultural occupa-
    tions.   In the Spanish-speaking West Indies, it is
    called a "machete."

MANCICATOEX.   Brother of Caonabo, who became lead-
    er of the Indian resistance to the Spaniards after
    Caonabo's capture.

MANES, THERAMENE.   Haitian composer, known for his
    use of Haitian folk rhythms, melodies and legends.

MANGER.   Creole term for sacrifice or feast.

MANGER MARASSA.   A sacrifice or feast for the spirit
    of twins.

MANGER MORTS.   A sacrifice or feast for the dead.

MANGER MOUN.   Literally, "to eat men."   This term

designates the fate of men who fall prey to malevolent spirits.

MANGER SEC. Minor offerings to voodoo dieties, usually food and drink, but not animal sacrifices.

MANGER-YAM. Two-day harvest festival in November each year. The words mean literally "eat yam." It is celebrated with feasting, drinking, dancing and singing. It is also a voodoo rite.

MANGONES, ALBERT. Haitian architect, credited with Robert Baussan, with having brought Haitian architecture from the classic French into simpler, more functional modern lines.

MANIOC (Cassava). A tuber plant used to make bread and starch. One of Haiti's principal crops.

MANNEVILLE. A small village on the northern shore of Lake Saumâtre, about 10 miles from the border with the Dominican Republic.

MARASSA. Twins, or the spirit of twins.

MARCELIN, PIERRE. Together with his brother Phillipe Thoby-Marcelin, Pierre Marcelin is the author of three novels of Haitian peasant life which were widely acclaimed in Haiti and abroad: Le Crayon de Dieu, Canapé-vert, and La Bête de Musseau.

MARCHATERRE. Small village near the city of Les Cayes, scene of the massacre of Haitian peasants by U.S. marines in December 1929. Accordingly, the name given to this incident.

MARECHAUSEE. A local police organization for general law enforcement and for the capture of fugitive slaves during the French colonial administration of Saint-Dominique.

MARIBAL VALLEY PROJECT. A UNESCO-supported community development project near Jacmel, 1948-

1950. It was intended to improve agricultural
methods, foster better health and combat illiteracy
in a proverty-stricken rural area. It had only
limited success, however, as a result of local
apathy, insufficient funds, corruption and the mag-
nitude of the task.

MARIGOT. Small village on the southern coast of Haiti.

MAROON. A slave who escaped into the mountainous interior of the island. In 1784, after an unsuccessful attempt to subdue by force the maroons hiding
in the Bahuruco Mountains, General Bellecombe acknowledged their independence.

MARRE. Tied or restrained, used to characterize a
voodoo spirit that has been tamed.

MARTINIQUE. African-type social dances associated
with rites for the dead.

MASSACRE RIVER (Rivière du Massacre, or Dajabon).
River on the Haiti-Dominican border flowing north
into the Atlantic Ocean.

MASSIAC CLUB. Reactionary group in France opposed
to the Club des Amis des Noirs, in other words,
preferring the continuation of slavery in French
colonies.

MASSIF DE LA HOTTE. Western portion of a mountain
range extending the full length of the southern peninsula of Haiti.

MASSIF DE LA SELLE. Eastern portion of a mountain
range which extends the full length of the southern
peninsula of Haiti. Several peaks have elevations
of over 7000 feet, and the Morne de la Selle at
8889 feet is the country's highest peak. Pine for-
ests on the higher slopes of this range constitute
the country's principal remaining timber resource.

MASSIF-DU-NORD. The most extensive of Haiti's mountain ranges, slanting southeastward from the Atlantic Ocean near Port-de-Paix to the Dominican border and beyond.

MATHON-BLANCHET, LINA. Collector, arranger and publisher of Haitian folksongs and dances.

MAUNDER CLAIM. This was a claim of a British citizen against the Haitian Government in the amount of $682,000. Each party accused the other of having violated terms for the exploitation of Turtle Island. It was finally settled for the payment of $154,000 under the guns of the H. M. S. Canada.

MAUREPAS. One of Toussaint L'Ouverture's more capable general officers. He resisted the French fiercely at Port-de-Paix and defeated the French general Debelle at the Battle of Trois Pavillons. But then he defected to the French, along with his entire regiment, when his situation looked hopeless. Later he and his family were tortured to death as the French commander, Rochambeau, went on his last rampage of death and destruction before evacuating the colony.

MAUVAISES AIRES. Synonym for LOUP GAROU.

MAY DECREE. Legislation passed by the French National Assembly in 1791 enfranchising all mulattoes born of free parents who met property qualifications. It came as a shock to the white colonists of Saint-Dominique and proved to be an opening wedge to the Haitian Revolution.

MAZON. Congo dance of Haitian origin.

MAZOUK. A lively dance resembling the Polish polka.

MERINGUE. The Haitian national social dance, resembling closely its Dominican counterpart.

MICHEL, ANTOINE. One of the most productive and highly reputed Haitian historians. He wrote ex-

tensively on politics in the Liberal era between the
rise of Geffard in 1859 and the fall of Boyer Baze-
lais in 1879.

MILICE CIVIL. The official name of the "ton-ton macoutes" until 1962.

MILLET. A grain grown on the dry plains and on stony
slopes, widely consumed in Haiti.

MILOT. Village about 11 miles south of Cap-Haïtien,
at the foot of La Ferrière mountain, site of the
ruins of Sans Souci palace.

MIRAGOANE. Small village on the northern shore of
Haiti's southern peninsula.

MIREBALAIS. Town in the central portion of Haiti on
the upper reaches of the Artibonite River.

MOLE-ST.-NICOLAS. A well-protected harbor on the
northeastern coast of Haiti which the United States
sought unsuccessfully to acquire in the late 19th
and early 20th century. German efforts to acquire
a naval base there was one of the reasons for the
U.S. intervention in Haiti in 1915.

MOLLENTHIEL, HILAIRE. One of Haiti's better-known
sculptors.

MONTAGNES NOIR. A mountain range extending lateral-
ly across the country to a point near the Artibonite
River.

MONTROUIS. Coastal town near the central part of Haiti.

MORISSEAU-LEROY, F. Haitian dramatist of the early
20th century who, with Frank Fouché, adapted the
classical works, Oedipus Rex and Antigone into
Creole.

MORNE LA PIERRE. Highest point (2500 feet) on the
Island of Gonâve in the Gulf of Gonâve.

MOTON, Dr. R. R.   Head of a U.S. Commission which
   investigated Haitian education.

MOUVEMENT D'OUVRIERS Y PAYSANS   see   WORKER-
   FARMER MOVEMENT

MOYSE (Moïse).   One of Toussaint L'Ouverture's most
   capable generals, and the most popular man in the
   Haitian army after Toussaint.
      Moyse came to the new world on a slave ship
   as a boy.   He was adopted by Toussaint, who passed him off as his nephew.   He stood high in Toussaint's favor during the first stages of the revolution, which brought Toussaint to power.   Toussaint
   named him commandant of the North Province, the
   most critical area of Haiti after Port-au-Prince,
   the capital.
      Moyse fell from favor when he refused to carry
   out Toussaint's severe labor reforms in North Province.   Cultivation in his district suffered.   Toussaint sent observers who reported that Moyse was
   openly critical of Toussaint's lenient policy toward
   whites and toward Toussaint's new constitution,
   which Moyse considered despotic.
      When a revolt broke out in North Province, with
   the aim of massacre of whites, break-up of their
   plantations, the overthrow of Toussaint, and his replacement by Moyse, Toussaint moved into the province with troops, had Moyse arrested and court-
   martialed, and when the tribunal acquitted him,
   Toussaint had his "nephew" marched to the town
   square and shot nevertheless.   The execution
   shocked the followers of Toussaint and Moyse.
   Toussaint went to great pains to try to justify the
   deed, but is said to have carried regrets over the
   precipitous act.   Moyse died gallantly, even giving
   command to fire at his own execution.

MULATTO.   A person of mixed black and white ances-
   try.   A good deal of Haitian history is based on
   struggles and rivalries among whites, blacks and
   mulattoes.   When Haiti attained its independence,
   the white elite was expelled and the mulattoes became the ruling class.

MUNRO, DANA G. (1892-   ).   U.S. High Commissioner
to Haiti, 1930-1934.   His primary task was liquid-
ation of the U.S. occupation of Haiti.

MUSEUM OF HAITIAN ART.   Part of the College of St.
Pierre on Heroes Square in Port-au-Prince, this
museum houses the finest permanent collection of
Haitian art.

- N -

NATIONAL ASSEMBLY.   The unicameral legislature of
Haiti, composed of 58 legislators with six-year
terms and eligibility for indefinite re-election.   In
order to be a member of the legislature, a candidate must be a Haitian citizen, at least 18 years
of age, enjoy full civil and political rights and have
resided at least five years in the district he seeks
to represent.

NATIONAL BANK.   The principal bank of Haiti.   Established by the French, it fell under the control of
the National City Bank of New York in 1919.
In 1921 it was rechartered as a Haitian corporation but it was not until 1947 that it was brought
under full control of the Haitian government.

NATIONAL COUNCIL FOR PLANNING AND DEVELOP-
MENT (Conseil National de Développement et de
Planification--CONADEP).   Government agency
charged with overall economic planning.   It was
created in 1963 as a result of assistance from the
Organization of American States, the United Nations
Economic Mission for Latin America and the Inter
American Development Bank.   It is headed by the
President of the Republic and is composed of the
secretaries of state for finance and economic affairs; public works, transportation and communication; commerce and industry; agriculture, natural
resources and rural development; and the president
of the National Bank of Haiti.

NATIONAL GUARD.   A gendarmerie established and

trained by the U.S. marines during the U.S. occupation of Haiti. A constabulary rather than an
army, it was nevertheless a highly efficient force,
well-trained and equipped. The force contributed
greatly to the reduction of rebellious activities in
the countryside.

NATIONAL OFFICE OF COMMUNITY EDUCATION
(ONEC). Agency of the Haitian Government, formed
in 1961 as a fusion between the urban adult education program and the rural community development
services of the Haitian Department of Agriculture.

NATIONAL PALACE.   The official residence of the Haitian Chief of State.

NATIONAL SECURITY VOLUNTEERS.   A civil militia,
composed mainly of rural peasants, organized by
President Duvalier as a counterpoise to the army.
They were estimated to number between 7000 and
10,000 men.

NATIONAL UNION OF HAITIAN WORKERS.   A labor fed-
eration which was banned by President François
Duvalier in 1958.

NATIONAL UNITY PARTY.   The only legal political party in contemporary Haiti.

NAVASSA.   A dry, barren island about a mile square located some 30 miles off Haiti's southwest coast.
In 1857, Peter Duncan, a Baltimore shipmaster,
took possession of the island under terms of the
U.S. Guano Islands Act of 1856, which specified
that "whenever a citizen of the United States dis-
covers a deposit of guano on any island ... not
within the lawful jurisdiction of any other Government, and takes peaceful possession thereof, and
occupies the same, such island ... may ... be
considered as appertaining to the United States. "
Digging began in 1858, whereupon Haiti declared
the island part of the Haitian empire. The U.S.
Saratoga was sent to protect the U.S. claim, and

digging continued until 1898, when the island was abandoned for fear of capture by the Spanish. In 1917, the United States erected a lighthouse on the island, since it posed a menace to shipping because of its location on the direct route to Panama.

The light was manned until 1929, when the U.S. Lighthouse Service, plagued by a series of tragedies to the keepers (one took his life, others suffered varying degrees of emotional disorder, and one was removed "a raving madman listening to voodoo drums"), refused to send any more men to such a remote and desolate spot. The light was made automatic, and it is now serviced every six months by the U.S. Coast Guard operating out of San Juan, Puerto Rico, and Miami.

The island remains uninhabited, except by goats, cats, rats, bats, lizards, and of course, thousands upon thousands of birds. Haiti still considers the island to be its possession, but has not pressed its claim, presumably because the island is now considered to have little commercial value and the Haitian Government is reluctant about taking over the expense and responsibility of servicing the lighthouse.

Navassa is kept under close surveillance by U.S. authorities as a suspected marijuana drop point. It is difficult to secure permission to visit the island. It is controlled by the Seventh Coast Guard District in Miami, which must give its approval. One must sign a document which reads in part, "I acknowledge that I understand that there are many dangers and hazards in visiting Navassa Island.... I do hereby, for myself, my heirs, executors, and administrators, remise, release and forever discharge ... the United States of America ... from any claim, demands on account of my death or on account of any injury to me which may occur from any cause."

NEGRITUDE. The glorification of the Afro-Haitian cultural legacy and the rejection of all things European.

NISSAGE-SAGET. President of Haiti from 1870 to 1874.

NORD-ALEXIS, PIERRE (1820-1910).   President of Haiti
    from 1902 to 1908.   Nord-Alexis, an octogenarian
    at the time, seized power in a surprise march on
    Port-au-Prince in 1902.   His administration was
    characterized by corruption, turmoil and distress.

NORMIL, ANDRE.   One of Haiti's better known contem-
    porary artists.

NORTHERN PLAIN.   An area of about 150 square miles
    located between the Atlantic Ocean and the Massif
    du Nord, extending from Cap-Haïtien to the Domin-
    ican border.   Its rich soil is formed by abrasion
    and by alluvial deposits.   It was the backbone of
    the economy in French colonial times.   It is ac-
    tually an extension of the rich Cibao Valley of the
    Dominican Republic.

NOVENA.   A nine-day ritual for the soul of one who has
    died, held on nine successive nights following the
    funeral.

- O -

OBIN, PHILOME (1891-   ).   Called the patriarch of Hai-
    ti's artistic renaissance, Philomé Obin, an octogen-
    arian, is still painting in Cap-Haïtien.

OBIN, SENEQUE.   Younger brother of Philomé Obin and
    a distinguished Haitian painter.

OEUVRES ESSENTIELLES.   Two-volume book by Fran-
    çois Duvalier which extols Negro-African civiliza-
    tion and preaches the gospel of racial pride.

OGAN.   An iron, usually a blade of a hoe, struck by a
    large spike during a voodoo dance.

OGE, VINCENT (ca. 1755-1791).   One of the commission-
    ers of the affranchis of Saint-Dominique in Paris.
    He returned to the island to assure the fair applica-
    tion of rights for the freedmen of Haiti but was cap--

tured by the French colonialists, tortured and put
to death.   With a companion Jean-Baptiste Chavon-
nes, their sentence read "whilst alive to have their
arms, legs, thighs and spines broken; and after-
ward to be placed on a wheel, their faces toward
heaven and there to stay as long as it would please
God to preserve their lives; and when dead, their
heads were to be cut off and exposed on poles. "
The sentence was carried out in public as ordered
on February 25, 1791.   The death of Ogé shook
France and forced the French National Assembly
to decree that henceforth all freedmen would be ad-
mitted to colonial assemblies.   This decree, which
angered the white colonists and inspired the gens
de couleur, sparked the revolution.   Later the
French administrators, in negotiations with rebellious slaves, were forced to declare the sentence
wrongful and promised to pay an indemity to his
widow and children.

OGUN (Ogoun).   The voodoo god of war.   Ogun's favorite color is said to be red, and he is said to "eat"
red cocks and red beans.

ONEC   see   NATIONAL OFFICE OF COMMUNITY EDU-
CATION

ORDINANCE OF 1825.   Ordinance by which King Charles
X of France granted the French part of Saint-Dominique (Haiti) its independence.   By this ordinance,
the French were obliged to pay only half duty on
their goods entering or leaving Haiti.   Haiti agreed
to pay an indemity of 150 million francs.   The ordinance drained Haiti of much of its resources.
The President of Haiti sought to renegotiate its
terms, and it was replaced in 1838 by a commercial treaty and convention.

ORESTE, MICHEL.   Senator, jurist and professor who
was elected President by the Haitian National Assembly in 1913.   He resigned after only eight
months in office in the face of a revolt.   In this
short period, he built up a considerable fund for

education but saw it dissipated for "military expenses" by the next administration.

OVANDO, NICOLAS.   Spanish Governor of the island of Hispaniola beginning on April 15, 1502.   He was most ruthless in his treatment of the Indians.

- P -

PADREJEAN.   Leader of a slave rebellion in Saint-Dominique in 1678, killed after inflicting heavy losses on the French.

PALAIS NATIONAL   see   NATIONAL PALACE

PANIER, JEAN.   Black commander who continued to resist French forces in Haiti, even after the surrender of Toussaint L'Ouverture and Dessalines.

PANNIER.   Woven saddle bags used by Haitian peasants to transport produce.

PAPALOI.   Term used in popular literature to designate a priest of voodoo, especially a healer.   A more precise term is houngan or hungan.

PAPA ZACA.   God of agriculture in the voodoo religion.

PAQUETS CONGO.   A small package, tightly wound, designed to protect a person against illness and evil spirits.

PATRIOTIC UNION (Union Patriotique).   Private organization formed in Haiti to try to bring an end to U.S. occupation of the country.

PE.   Small altar to a voodoo god.   Also called sabagui.

PEDERNALES RIVER.   On the Haiti-Dominican border flowing south into the Caribbean Sea.

PELIGRE DAM.   Built at a cost of $30 million and located near the border of the Dominican Republic, Peligré Dam is the highest in the world and holds back 328 million cubic meters of water, which is used for irrigation as well as for the generation of electricity.

PELLETIER, ANTONIO. A native of France, whose U.S. citizenship was in doubt. He roamed the Caribbean as an adventurer and was finally apprehended for piracy by Haitian authorities. He was sentenced to five years in prison but escaped and presented a claim for wrongs suffered, which ultimatedly reached the total of $2,466,480. The claim dragged on through several U.S. and Haitian administrations and embittered relations between the two countries until finally dismissed in 1866.

PENATES. According to voodoo belief, gods who protect the household and the nation.

PENITENCE. Special clothing worn to comply with a vow made to a voodoo god, or to please the god, usually in the god's own sacred colors.

PERALTE, CHARLEMAGNE. A caco chief who was convicted by a U.S. occupation court of complicity in an attack on the gendarmerie in 1917. He escaped in 1918 and led resistance against U.S. occupation. He was killed in October, 1918.

PERISTYLE. The roofed, open-sided area of a voodoo temple, where most of the dancing and ceremonies take place.

PESTEL. Small village on the northern shore of Haiti's southern peninsula.

PETERS, DEWITT. U.S. artist who, as teacher of English in a Haitian government school, is generally credited with having stimulated the Haitian school of primitive art.

PETION, ALEXANDER (1770-1818). Called the "Pan-

americanist, " Alexander Pétion was President of
the West Department of Haiti from 1807 to 1818.
He was concerned with the liberation of slaves
everywhere and provided Simón Bolívar with wea-
pons and munitions on the promise that he, Bolí -
var, would abolish slavery in the parts of South
America that he liberated.

Pétion was born in Port-au-Prince in 1770, the
son of a black mother and white French jeweler.
Educated in Paris, he fled to France when Toussaint conquered South Province and returned with
Le Clerc in the latter's expedition against the
blacks in 1802.   When Napoleon started to discrim-
inate against mulattoes, Pétion joined the cause of
the blacks.   He participated in the Haitian declaration at Gonaïves, took an oath of allegiance to Dessalines, and was placed in command at Port-au-
Prince.   As a military man, he tended to be mild-
tempered and conciliatory rather than aggresive
like Christophe and Dessalines.

Pétion founded an oligarchic republic, which
pleased the mulatto elite.   In practice he exercised
dictatorial powers.   He professed democratic ideals
and allowed the people unprecedented liberty.   He
confiscated the large French plantations and par-
celed out small plots to soldiers and officers.   In
so doing he changed the entire agricultural base
of Haitian society, from that of export crops (coffee, indigo, sugar, etc.) to subsistence farming.
He died on March 29, 1818.

PETIONVILLE.   A suburb of Port-au-Prince, at a higher altitude than the city (500 meters) and thus much
cooler, where most resort hotels are located and
most well-to-do people live.   It is 17 kilometers
from Port-au-Prince and has a population of about
10, 000.

PETIT BLANC.   A white person not of the elite (for example shopkeepers, artisans, small planters) during the French colonial period.   Considerable an-
tagonism existed between the petit blancs (minor
whites) and grands blancs (important whites), who

were the wealthy ruling class.

PETIT-GOAVE. Small coastal town about 50 miles southwest of Port-au-Prince, the capital.

PETIT-NOEL. Black commander who continued to resist the French, even after the surrender of Toussaint L'Ouverture and Dessalines.

PETIT-TROU-DE-NIPPES. Small village on the northern shore of Haiti's southern peninsula.

PETRO. One of two principal groups of voodoo dieties, and thus the rites associated with this group. The word is said to come from the name of a powerful voodoo priest of the Haitian pre-revolutionary period.

PHILADELPHIA CIRCLE. A society in Cap-Français which devoted itself to politics, philosophy and literature during the French colonial era.

PHILOLOGIE CREOLE. One of the first linguistic studies of Haitian creole, written by Jules Faine in 1936.

PIERRE, ANDRE. One of Haiti's better known contemporary artists.

PIERRE-LOUIS, NEMOURS. President of the Supreme Court of Haiti who headed a provisional government for one month and 10 days toward the end of 1956 and the beginning of 1957.

PIERROT, GENERAL JEAN LOUIS (1761-1846). President of Haiti from April 16, 1845, to March 24, 1846. He was illiterate and easily manipulated by the mulatto elite. He was forced from office by the Haitian Council of State largely because of the failure of his military campaigns to reassert Haitian rule over Santo Domingo.

PINCHINAT, PIERRE. One of the leaders of the Haitian Revolution. A mulatto, he had the benefits of a

French education and a strong hatred for whites.
He was more of a politician and negotiator than a
field commander.

PIQUET. Mountaineers in the southern part of Haiti who
were often called upon to form the mercenaries and
fill the ranks of insurrectionist movements.

PIQUETS WAR. A peasant rebellion which began in 1843
in the southern peninsula of Haiti under the leadership of the peasant, Acaau.

PLACAGE. A social substitute for marriage. A man
and a woman who wish to live together take on
certain obligations and go through a simple ceremony at the home of the woman's parents.

PLACEE. A person living with another person as man
or wife without the blessings of a legal ceremony.

PLAINE DE L'ARTIBONITE. The plain formed by the
Valley of the Artibonite River between the Montagnes Noires to the north and the Chaîne de Mateau to the south.

PLAINE DU NORD. Plain in the northeast near Cap-
Haïtien where, in colonial times, lay most of the
flourishing French plantations and palatial residen-
ces, and where the slave insurrection began in
1791.

PLANTAIN. A starchy-type of banana used for cooking.
One of Haiti's principal crops.

PLATEAU CENTRAL. A relatively flat region in the center of Haiti between the Massif du Nord to the
north and the Montagnes Noires to the south.

PLAT-MARASSA. The plate of food offered to divine
twins.

POLVEREL, ETIENNE. A French Civil Commissioner
of Saint-Dominique who freed the slaves in the

southern and western portions of the island in the period 1792-1794. He was largely eclipsed by fellow-commissioner, Félicité Sonthonax, but they worked together in trying to extirpate royal influence from Saint-Dominique. Both were called to France to stand trial before the National Convention for exceeding their powers. They were both acquitted, however, and given seats in the Convention.

POPULATION.   There are no reliable census figures for Haiti.   Estimates of total population range from 3. 5 million to 5. 1 million.   This would indicate an average population density of 317 to 477 persons per square mile, high by world standards but average for the Caribbean.   But when one remembers that this population resides, for the most part, in the limited area of the valleys and coastal plain, Haiti is greatly overpopulated in terms of habitable land.   The rate of population growth is 2. 4 percent, again about average for the Caribbean.

Nearly all the population lives in rural areas. Port-au-Prince, the capital and largest city, has a population of only 350, 000. Number two in size is Cap-Haïtien in the north with a population of 35, 000.

Haiti is the most African of the Caribbean islands. Estimates of pure Negroes run as high as 95 percent, with most of the remainder mulatto descendants of early French colonists who mixed with Africans.

Infant mortality is estimated at 190 per thousand, at least double the average for Latin America. The median age of the population is about 19 years. Life expectancy is estimated at about 47 for females and 49 for males, suggesting a fairly high rate of maternal mortality.

Haiti is thought to lose as many as 20, 000 persons a year through emigration. Over 200, 000 are believed to be living in the Dominican Republic, most of them illegally. Another 200, 000 are believed to be in Canada, the United States, the Bahamas and Venezuela.

PORT-AU-PRINCE.   Capital of Haiti.   Population, 350,000.   Founded in 1749 by the French, it has been the capital of Haiti since 1808.

PORT-DE-PAIX.   Chief town in the Department of the Northwest.

PORT MARGOT.   Village on the western end of Hispaniola founded by French and English buccaneers in 1641, giving them their first claim to the mainland.

PORTO [or POTEAU] CABESSE [or LEGBA or MITA(N)]. The central post of the tonnelle which the voodoo gods are said to descend when summoned at a voodoo ceremony.

PORT REPUBLICAINE.   Early name for Port-au-Prince.

PORT-SALUT.   Small town on the southern shore of Haiti.

POTEAU MITAN.   Central post of a voodoo temple. According to voodoo belief, the gods or spirits enter the temple by descending this pole.

POT TETE.   The covered pot in which, according to voodoo belief, spirits are kept.

POUA.   Creole term for "bean."   There are many varieties grown in Haiti, of which the poua rouj (red bean), poua nouva (black bean) and poua blá (white bean) are the most common.

POUIN.   According to voodoo belief, a powerful protective charm.

POWELL, WILLIAM F.   The U.S. Minister to Haiti beginning in 1897.   He devoted himself to promoting trade between Haiti and the United States and encouraging U.S. investment in Haiti.   His object was to create Haitian dependency on the United States.

PREFET.   Governor of an arrondissement.

PRESIDENTIAL PALACE. The home and office of
the President of Haiti, located in downtown Port-
au-Prince. It is also used to house troops and
as a depot for arms and ammunition.

PRET' SAVAN'. Learned priest of any sect, usually
of the interior of the country. Savan' has the
meaning of both a "learned person" and "savannah"
or "plains. " In the latter sense, it has come to
mean all interior regions. Also, a term applied
to the person who reads or recites Catholic liturgy
at a voodoo ceremony.

PREVOST, JULIAN see LIMONADE, COMTE DE

PRICE-MARS, Jean (1876-). Haitian historian and
ethnologist who resurrected Haitian folklore and
extolled its values. First director of the Haitian Bureau of Ethnology, later a senator and
Haitian representative to the United Nations, Dr.
Price-Mars wrote the first anthropological study
of Haiti, Ainsi parla l'oncle (1928). It tended
to romanticize the Haitian peasant and proved
a stimulant toward further research and self-
identification.

PRIERE GUINEE. The prayer in a voodoo ceremony.

PRIX-DES-YEUX. Literally, "prize" or "price" of the
eyes, this is the designation given to the highest
degree of voodoo initiates, presumably because the
innermost secrets of the cult are now revealed to
them.

PUBLIQUE. A "public car," providing economical transportation. Publiques travel fixed routes but do not
have fixed schedules.

PUBLIQUES LAIQUES. Primary schools operated by the
Government of Haiti.

- Q -

QUARTIER-MORIN.   Village in the North Department of
    Haiti and in the arrondissement of Cap-Haïtien.

QUILOMBO.   A village community built by African-born
    emancipated slaves on the basis of the extended
    family.   The object was to satisfy the basic needs
    of the group.   Merchandizing of labor, food or
    land was not attempted.   Wealth consisted of the
    accumulation of real property.

QUISQUEYA.   Early Indian name for the island now known
    as Hispaniola.

- R -

RADA.   One of the two principal groups of voodoo dieties
    and thus the rites associated with this group.

RAIMOND, JULIEN.   Leader, with Vincent Ogé, of a
    mulatto pressure group in Paris at the time of the
    French Revolution.   Later he was appointed a
    French commissioner to Saint-Dominique.

RAMIE.   A perennial plant of the nettle family, grown
    in Haiti for its strong, lustrous fibers.

RAPADOU.   A syrup produced when refining sugar.   It
    is the basis for clairin, which is raw Haitian rum.

RARA.   Band of torch bearers and religious worshippers
    organized in particular during Holy Week.

RARA BAND.   A carnival dance group.

RAVIN-A-COULEUVRE   see   SNAKE GULLEY

RAYNAL, ABBE.   French priest who called for a slave
    revolution in his book, Philosophical and Political
    History of the Establishments and Commerce in the

Two Indies. It is said that Toussaint L'Ouverture was much influenced by this book, which called for a courageous chief to lead the black movement toward freedom.

REGULATIONS RELATIVE TO THE CULTURE. Regulations proclaimed by Toussaint L'Ouverture for the purpose of keeping the peasants under tight military control.

RENAUD. Mulatto commander and one of André Rigaud's most capable subordinate officers. He fought off the British successfully in South Province in 1796.

RENVOYER. The banishing of a voodoo god who has been troublesome.

REPARTIMIENTOS. The system of dividing land and assigning slaves to Spanish settlers, begun by Columbus in 1496.

RETIRER D'EN BAS DE L'EAU. Voodoo ceremony for reclaiming the souls of the deceased from the deep waters to which they have descended.

REVADEZ. Small retailer.

REYNOLDS METAL COMPANY. Major U.S. aluminum corporation which contracted to exploit Haitian bauxite.

RICHARD, JEAN PIERRE. Duke of Marmelade in the Kingdom of Henri Christophe. When the king was incapacitated by a stroke, the Duke led a revolt against him.

RICHE, JEAN-BAPTISTE (1785-1847). President of Haiti from March 1, 1846, to February 27, 1847. He promulgated a new constitution in 1846 but died before he could put it into practice.

RIGAUD, ANDRE. Leader of the free blacks and mulattoes in the south of Saint-Dominique in the 1790's

and a rival of Toussaint L'Ouverture. He shares
with Toussaint credit for driving the British from
the colony. The British attempted to bribe Rigaud
with an offer of 3 million francs which he rejected
with scorn.

Rigaud was born in Les Cayes on January 17, 1761,
of a black mother and white French father. He is
said to have fought in Savannah with the French
during the American Revolution. After the war he
returned to Saint-Dominique, where he was a gold-
smith until the outbreak of the Haitian Revolution.
He died at Les Cayes on September 17, 1811.

Rigaud personified the mulatto drive for vengeance
and saw little use for whites or blacks. Thus he
never achieved the strength and unity that Toussaint
attained in the north. Rigaud waged war for 14
months against Toussaint in an unsuccessful effort
to gain control of South Province.

RIO DAJABON   see   MASSACRE RIVER

RIVIERE DU MASSACRE   see   MASSACRE RIVER

ROCHAMBEAU, GENERAL DONATIEN (1750-1815). Le
Clerc's second-in-command and later successor as
commander of French forces in Saint-Dominique,
1802-1803.

Rochambeau considered blacks inferior to ani-
mals and proceeded to slaughter the black population of the colony. Some were taken to sea, gas-
sed and drowned. Savage dogs were imported from
Cuba and turned loose against them.

The blacks fought back with a fanaticism border-
ing on suicide. Rochambeau's forces were driven
back from the interior until he held only Cap-
Français and Môle-St.-Nicolas. Some of his final
days in Saint-Dominique were passed in sexual or-
gies, military balls and banquets. On November
19, 1803, he signed a truce with the black general
Dessalines, agreeing to evacuate Cap-Français.
He surrendered to the British fleet lying off shore.
With the surrender of the French garrison at Môle-
St.-Nicolas a few days later, Saint-Dominique was

at last free of French domination. The black population of Haiti had been reduced from about half
a million in 1791 to only about 350,000.

ROLDAN-JIMENEZ. Leader of malcontent Spaniards on
the island of Hispaniola. Columbus granted to
Roldán and his followers a certain quantity of land
and a sufficient number of Indians to cultivate it,
thus establishing slavery for the first time in the
Western Hemisphere.

ROMAIN, JACQUES B. Haitian poet, novelist and writer. His book, Gouverneurs de la Rosée (Masters
of the Dew), published in 1944, a realistic portrayal of life in a peasant community, has been trans-
lated into 17 languages. He was founder of the
Haitian Communist Party and the Bureau of Ethnology. He stimulated the study of Haiti's African
roots. He died in 1943 at the age of 36.

ROUMAIN, ERNEST. First Haitian diplomatic representative to the United States, in 1862, he held the
title of chargé d'affaires.

ROUME, PHILIPPE. French agent, first in Santo Domingo, then Cap-Français. He turned out to be a
rubber stamp for Toussaint L'Ouverture's acts.
At L'Ouverture's insistence, he was removed by
the French Directory in 1801.

ROUMER, EMILE. Haitian poet who wrote in the French
language but in Creole style and sentiment.

ROY, EUGENE. Private Haitian banker who was chosen
interim President of Haiti in 1930 for the express
purpose of supervising the election of a new National Assembly. The task completed, he resigned
as promised and the assembly chose Stenio Vincent
as his successor.

ROYAL DAHOMETS. Twenty thousand black troops,
carefully selected from Africa and vigorously trained, who not only served as a body guard to Henri

Christophe but also served as an internal police
force and informer system during his reign.

RURAL CODE.   Part of the Code Henri of King Henri
Christophe which applied to agriculture.   It regulated hours and conditions of work, duties of plantation owners and laborers, supervision of plantations and the cultivation of crops.   The code required that one-fourth of production be given to
laborers.   Workers were tied to the soil like serfs,
but were better off than under slavery.

Also, a law of 1826 promulgated by President
Boyer which applied to all of Haiti and required
every Haitian except for aristocrats, officers and
artisans and soldiers to till the land.   A rural police force supervised implementation of the code.
It proved impossible to enforce, however, since
the peasants had become used to indolence and Haiti lacked the administrative machinery to insure
compliance.

In 1959-60, François Duvalier attempted to in-
troduce a new Rural Code to grant a degree of
civil government to rural sections, but dissension
in the legislature postponed its implementation.

RURAL SECTION.   The smallest unit of local government in Haiti.

RUSSELL, GENERAL JOHN H.   First U. S. High Commissioner to Haiti, 1922-1930.   He ruled Haiti as
a virtual dictator in collaboration with Haitian President Luis Borno.

General Russell was a Georgian who had commanded the Marines in Haiti in the wars against
the cacos.   He was not very sophisticated in the
art of government, but he was firm, honest and
a born disciplinarian.

RYSWICK, TREATY OF.   Treaty which in 1697 ended
the war in Europe between France on the one hand
and Austria, Spain, Sweden, England and a number
of German states on the other.   Part of this treaty
gave France clear title to the western part of the

island of Hispaniola, in other words, the area now
known as Haiti.

- S -

SABAGUI see PE

SAGET, NISSAGE. President of Haiti from March 19,
1870, to May 14, 1874. He died on April 7, 1880.
He was one of only three presidents before the
U. S. intervention to remain in office until the end
of his term. Most of his time was devoted to problems arising from relations with the neighboring
Dominican Republic, where a civil war raged, and
to foreign claims against the Haitian Government.

ST. -AUDE, MAGLOIRE. Haitian poet who wrote in
French but in Creole style and sentiment.

SAINT-DOMINIQUE (Sainte Dominique). Name of Haiti
while under French rule. Saint-Dominique became
one of the richest colonies of the New World. Arts
and letters and nobility developed second only to
the cultural centers of Europe.
On attaining independence, the black revolutionary leaders of Saint-Dominique decided to call their
new nation Haiti, after the original Indian name for
the island.
Under French rule, Saint-Dominique flourished
as a center of coffee, cotton, cacao, tobacco, indigo and sugar production. Highways, sugar mills,
and elaborate irrigation systems were constructed
to serve the plantations, based on slave labor.
By 1742, the sugar production of Saint-Dominique
exceeded that of all the British West Indies com-
bined. By 1783 its commerce constituted more
than a third of all French foreign trade.

SAINTE-TRINITE. An Episcopal cathedral in downtown
Port-au-Prince especially famous for its murals.
They recount the Biblical story as interpreted by
some of Haiti's most famous artists.

ST. JOHN, SIR SPENCER (1825-1910). British minister
to the Republic of Haiti from 1865 to 1871, who
gave impetus to a new school of sensational report-
ing on events in Haiti. His Hayti, or the Black
Republic was notorious for its distortion and mis-
representation of Haitian society and culture, especially the rites of voodoo.

SAINT-LEGER. French peace commissioner to Saint-
Dominique in 1792. He tried in vain to mend white
disunity (between petits blancs and grand blancs)
in the colony.

SAINT-MARC. City in Haiti north of Port-au-Prince
with a population of about 10,000.

SAINT-MARC COLONIAL ASSEMBLY. An assembly of
"patriots" (petits blancs) in the town of Saint-Marc
in 1790. It drafted a constitution for the colony
of Saint-Dominque which recognized the crown as
superior authority but otherwise gave autonomy to
the colony. They were opposed by the grands
blancs of the Northern Province. Civil war was
averted when the Assembly agreed to adjourn and
sent 85 delegates to France to plead its case before the French National Assembly. The patriots'
strategy failed when the National Assembly sided
with the grands blancs.

SAINT-RAPHAEL. Village in the north-central part of
Haiti.

SAINTS. Voodoo gods and goddesses.

SALNAVE, SYLVAIN MAJOR (1827-1870). Aided by
sympathizers from the Dominican Republic, Salnave
seized Cap-Haïtien and held the city from May 9 to
November 9, 1865. On May 6, 1867 he was elected President of Haiti. He forcibly ejected the
members of the House of Representatives, suspen-
ded the Constitution and had himself declared President-for-Life. This raised opposition in the country, which he sought to crush by force. Too late,

he appointed a legislative council and sought to liberalize the government. He was court-martialed and shot on January 15, 1870.

SALOMON, LOUIS ETIENNE FELICITE LYSIUS (1820-1888). President of Haiti from October 23, 1879, to August 10, 1888. He attempted both monetary and agricultural reforms without success. He did improve communications with the outside world through the laying of a submarine cable. He was opposed by the mulattoes, whom he executed in great numbers. When he tried to extend his tenure beyond the constitutional limit, he was faced with a civil war and chose exile in France.
    Salomon was a Francophile. He had a white French wife and a mulatto daughter. With the aid of French capital, he founded the Banque National d'Haiti. He accepted a French military mission and French teachers. His outstanding contribution was the liquidation of Haiti's debt to France.

SAM, VILBRUN GUILLAUME. He established himself as President of Haiti in 1915 but was immediately driven from office by a rival faction. He fled to the French legation but a mob dragged him from the premises, tore his body apart and marched through the city with the pieces. This led to a landing by U.S. marines.

SANDERS, PRINCE. A U.S. black educated at Moor's Charity School at Dartmouth College in 1807 and 1808. He was active in helping his fellow blacks in the United States. At the suggestion of English abolitionists, he went to Haiti to help organize schools and further Protestantism. He was impressed by Christophe and became a staunch supporter of his regime. In 1816, he published Haytian Papers in London. Two years later, a U.S. edition was released in Boston. It is said that Sanders brought vaccine to Haiti and personally vaccinated Christophe's children.

SANS SOUCI. A magnificent palace of yellow stone near

Cap-Haïtien, built by King Henri Christophe. It
lies in ruins today. Christophe was an admirer
of German technology and had Sans Souci built as
an exact replica of the Potsdam Palace constructed
by Frederick II of Prussia. The palace has three
stories with 23 windows each and is surrounded by
17 acres of gardens. It was badly damaged by an
earthquake in 1842, but the shell of the building
still stands.

Christophe was crowned in Sans Souci and took
his own life in the palace, after suffering a stroke
and being unable to suppress a rebellion.

SANTA MARIA. Flagship of Christopher Columbus, the
remains of which are believed to lie on a reef ad-
jacent to the city of Cap-Haïtien.

SAUNDERS, PRINCE see SANDERS

SCYLLA. Black commander who continued to resist
French forces in Haiti even after the surrender of
Toussaint L'Ouverture and Dessalines.

SECONDE. The middle-sized drum in the trio of voodoo
drums.

SEKRETE. A person who handles money and directs the
affairs of another person.

SERVICE. A voodoo ritual.

SERVICE TECHNIQUE DE L'AGRICULTURE ET DE L'
ENSEIGNEMENT PROFESSIONAL. A service organized in 1924 under the U.S. occupation as a
bureau in the Haitian Ministry of Agriculture. Its
principal functions were to provide higher agricultural education for the training of experts, research
workers, teachers of farm schools, and farm ad-
visers; rural farm schools, advice to farmers, and
(through animal clinics and demonstrations) experi-
ments in all phases of agricultural activity and vocational industrial education. The Service Technique
sought to persuade the peasants to diversify their
crops.

The Service was bitterly opposed by the elite
who correctly saw an educated peasantry as a threat
to their privileged position. The Service made an
important contribution to the development of a Haitian yeomanry.

SESAME. An herb grown in Haiti, whose small flat
seeds are a source of oil and a flavoring agent.

SHADA (Société Haitienne-Américaine de Développement)
see HAITIAN-AMERICAN DEVELOPMENT ASSO-
CIATION

SIMCOE, JOHN. British general who arrived in Saint-
Dominique on February 28, 1797, and commanded
a British force of 30,000 men. He was unable to
make progress against the forces of Toussaint
L'Ouverture and assumed defensive positions along
the coast until the arrival of General Thomas Maitland in 1798.

SIMIDOR. Leader of song at a combite.

SIMON, ANTOINE. President of Haiti from December
17, 1908, to Agust 2, 1911. He was preoccupied
with trying to solve Haiti's financial crises during
this period. He was overthrown by Cincinnatus
Leconte in 1911 and died in 1912.

SIMON-SAM, TIRESIAS. President of Haiti from 1896
to 1902. Simon Sam insisted that his term ran
until 1903, but he was persuaded to relinquish the
Presidency in 1902. He is best known for his resistance to German claims.

SISAL. A plant whose fibers are used to make twine
and rope, also hats, shoes, handbags, curtains and
carpets. The plant was introduced into Haiti in
1927 and is one of the country's principal cash
crops.

SLAVE. A black in bondage. Slaves constituted about
90 percent of the populations of pre-revolutionary
Haiti (about half a million) at the end of the 18th

century. They rose in rebellion against their white
masters, killing and ravaging throughout the countryside. Slaves were treated, with few exceptions, with
savage and inhuman cruelty. They labored from
dawn to dusk under the whips of their overseers.
The slightest insubordination resulted in severe
punishment, such as cutting off ears or tongues or
being nailed to a wall.

SNAKE GULLY. Scene, seven miles from Gonaïves, of
an ambush of the French General Rochambeau by
Toussaint L'Ouverture in 1802. Thousands of men
died on both sides in the battle that ensued.

SOCIETE CONGO. A tightly organized cooperative work
group found in certain parts of Haiti, a counterpart
to the more loosely organized combite.

SOCIETY OF FRIENDS OF THE BLACKS (La Société des
Amis des Noirs) see AMIS DES NOIRS

SONTHONAX, LEGER FELICITE. French Civil Commissioner in Haiti who proclaimed freedom for the
slaves in August 1793. He was forced to leave
Haiti in 1797 as a result of the intrigues of Toussaint L'Ouverture.
    Sonthonax was a Jacobin who became associated
with the Amis des Noirs. He was determined to
eradicate the last vestige of royalism from Saint-
Dominique. He allied himself first with the mulattoes and then, in time of crisis, offered freedom
to all black insurgents who would fight for him.
In negotiations with Toussaint, Sonthonax, a white,
advocated independence for Saint-Dominique and extermination of all whites. He was recalled by the
French legislature because of his "excesses."
    Sonthonax failed to make effective use of either
the whites or the blacks. He considered whites to
be the enemies of the French Revolution. Instead
of using their talents, he harassed and exiled them.
He was very permissive toward the blacks. As a
result, he was not able to get much work out of
them.

SORGHUM. A grain grown on the dry plains and on stony slopes that is widely consumed in Haiti.

SOULOUQUE, FAUSTIN (1785-1867). President of Haiti from March 1, 1847, to August 28, 1849, and Emperor from August 29, 1849, to January 15, 1859. He twice sought to subdue the Spanish portion of the island. Opposed by forces of General Fabre Nicolas Geffard, he fled the country in 1859. An illiterate former chief of the presidential guard, Soulouque set aside the constitution and ruled through terror and secret, quasi-military groups. Corruption and administrative inefficiency were characteristics of his regime.

SYLVAIN, FRANCK. Head of a provisional government in Haiti for two months in 1957.

SYLVAIN, GEORGES. Editor of The Anthology of Haitian Literature (1925).

- T -

TAFIA. A rum made from distilled sugar cane juice.

TAINO. Indian tribe of Arawak origin which inhabited Hispaniola at the time of its discovery by Columbus. Originally believed to number over a million, they were decimated to about 60,000 in 1508 and 500 in 1548.

TAP-TAP. Colloquial word (derived from the sound of the engine) for a gaily colored truck used for the conveyance of passengers. A wooden frame is constructed over a truck chassis and benches installed to increase passenger-carrying capacity. They carry various religious, humorous or philosophical names, such as "Angel of God," "God Bless You," or "For the Love of God."

TASSOT. A tasty preparation of meat (usually beef, turkey or pork) which has been dried on a hot tin roof, marinated for 24 hours and grilled over a charcoal fire.

THELEMAQUE, GENERAL SEIDE. A northern mulatto who rose to power under President Salnave. He led a successful revolution against President Salomon in 1888 but was killed in fighting in Port-au-Prince that same year.

THEODORE, DAVILMER. President of Haiti for four months in 1915. He fell from power because of insufficient funds to pay his caco followers.

THOBY-MARCELIN, PHILIPPE. Author, together with his brother, Pierre Marcelin, of three novels widely acclaimed in Haiti and abroad: Le Crayon de Dieu, Canapé-vert and La Bête de Musseau.

THOMAS, JANVIER. Black commander who continued to resist French forces in Haiti even after the surrender of Toussaint L'Ouverture and Dessalines.

TI-BON-ANGE. The conscience of a person.

TI-MOUN. A social institution of quasi-adoption whereby children, often the off-spring of peasants who do not have the means to care for them, are given to friends who live in town for their rearing and upbringing. The child repays the cost of upkeep by helping in the garden and running errands. When the child is older, he returns to his own home.

TONNELLE. Covered area of a voodoo temple, usually thatched with branches of palm trees.

TONNERRE, BOISROND. Author of the Haitian Declaration of Independence.

TON-TON MACOUTES. Literally, "bogey men." These were the secret police created by President François Duvalier. With a license to kill in the President's name and acting as informers, they were generally feared by the populace. In order to generate greater acceptance for his regime, Presi-

dent Jean-Claude Duvalier abolished the dreaded
Ton-Ton Macutes in 1971.

TORTUGA   see   TURTLE ISLAND

TOUSSAINT L'OUVERTURE.   A slave who became the
   savior of his country.   Born in 1743, he showed
   so much aptitude that his kindly master gave him
   leisure to develop his mind.   Toussaint considered
   himself selected by God to lead his fellow blacks
   to freedom.   In 1794, following the Spanish invasion of Saint-Dominique, Toussaint was commander
   of 4000 blacks in the Spanish service in Saint-Dominique.   He deserted with his troops to lead the
   native black rebellion.   With his defection, the
   Spanish invasion collapsed.   He then turned his at-
   tention to British invaders, whose ranks were decimated by yellow fever, driving the remnants of
   their forces from the island.
      In 1801 Toussaint promulgated a constitution for
   Saint-Dominique which designated him Governor
   General for life with the power of designating his
   successor.   The Constitution acknowledged French
   sovereignty in a perfunctory way and in effect
   placed control of all Hispaniola in the hands of
   Toussaint.
      Napoleon Bonaparte was both envious and jealous
   of his black rival in the Caribbean and despatched
   his brother-in-law, General Charles Victor Emmanuel Le Clerc, with 20,000 veteran troops to the
   colony to bring Toussaint to heel.   After prolonged
   resistance, Toussaint submitted on condition that
   he be allowed to retire peacefully on one of his
   estates.   When an epidemic of yellow fever virtual-
   ly decimated Le Clerc's forces, the latter became
   fearful of Toussaint, captured him and sent him to
   France, where he died of consumption in a French
   dungeon on April 7, 1803.
      Much has been written about Toussaint.   It is
   said that he acquired the nom-de-guerre L'Ouverture because of his ability to find or create open-
   ings in the lines of his enemies.   "Ouverture" in
   French means "opening."   Some historians consider

him the nation's foremost hero and the George
Washington of his country. In 11 short years he
led his people from misery to security, driving
out three major invaders. On the other hand, he
was a supreme schemer, playing off one element
against another, defecting to the strongest center
of power in order to retain authority. He was al-
ternately conciliatory and ruthless. He forced the
former slaves into a system of corvée which he
administered with strict discipline and force.
Nevertheless, he commanded the fierce loyalty of
his fellow blacks and the respect of all his enemies.

TRAITEMENT. Healing through the use of herbs and
magic.

TREATY OF RYSWICK (1697) see RYSWICK, TREATY
OF

TROIS RIVIERES. The second longest river of Haiti
(the first is the Artibonite). It empties into the
Atlantic at the town of Port-de-Paix.

TRONE. The altar at a voodoo service.

TROUIN. Small village about 30 miles southwest of Port-
au-Prince, the capital.

TURNIER, LUCE. Contemporary Haitian artist of considerable reknown.

TURTLE ISLAND (also called, in French, Ile de la Tortue, or simply, La Tortue; in Spanish, La Tortuga). A small island (70 square miles) off Haiti's
northern coast, which was the haunt of pirates and
buccaneers. It was first settled by the French and
English in 1625 and was used by the French as a
springboard from which to occupy the western part
of Hispaniola. In 1640, the French drove the English from the island, thus marking France's first
claim to Saint-Dominique.

- U -

UNIFIED PARTY OF HAITIAN COMMUNISTS (Parti Uni-
fié des Communistes Haïtiens). Haitian Communist
Party, formed in 1969 by the merger of the Parti
d' Entente Populaire and the Parti Populaire de
Liberation Nationale.

UNIH. National Union of Haitian Teachers. Created in
1946, it was open to teachers of primary, secondary and higher education. UNIH advocated pupil
democratization of education, a balanced and ra-
tional curriculum, vocational training, school caf-
eterias, free and compulsory school medical ex-
aminations, a law governing the teaching profession,
improved teacher training, more school inspectors,
better buildings and nationalization of Presbyterian
schools. It has since gone out of existence.

UNION PATRIOTIQUE see PATRIOTIC UNION

UNIVERSITY OF HAITI. Haiti's single university, established in Port-au-Prince in 1944. It is made up
of seven faculties and a School of Higher International Studies. The faculties are (1) agronomy,
(2) arts and sciences, (3) medicine and pharmacy,
(4) dentistry, (5) education and letters, (6) law and
administration, (7) ethnology. In recent years, en-
rollment has varied between one and two thousand.

UNSANKON see ADJANIKON

- V -

VALCIN, GERARD. One of Haiti's better known contemporary artists.

VALEMO, ALEXIS. Black commander who continued to
resist French forces in Haiti even after the surrender of Toussaint L'Ouverture and Dessalines.

VALENTIN, POMPEE   see   VASTEY, BARON DE

VASTEY, BARON DE.   Private Secretary, friend and
    advisor to King Henri Christophe.   He was other-
    wise known as Pompée Valentin.   A mulatto edu-
    cated in France, he hated whites with a vengeance.
    He was extremely loyal to King Henri and was one
    of the chief defenders of the monarchy.   Among
    his principal works, written under the name of
    Baron de Vastey, were Le Systeme colonial devoilé
    (Cap Henry, 1814), Reflexions politiques sur les
    noirs et les blancs (Cap Henry, 1816), Reflexions
    politiques sur quelques ouvrages et governaux fran-
    çais concernant Hayti (Sans Souci, 1817), and Essai
    sur les causes de la revolution et des guerres civ-
    iles d'Hayti (Sans Souci, 1819).

VERRETTES.   Village in the central part of Haiti on the
    Artibonite River.

VERTIERES, BATTLE OF.   Scene of final victory of the
    Haitians over the French during the Haitian Revo-
    lution.

VERVERS (Vevers).   A symbolic drawing of a voodoo
    god, traced on the ground using either flour or
    ashes or both.

VIEN-VIEN.   Creole term for ghost.

VIEUX, DAMOCLES.   Diplomat, poet and first director
    of the Teacher Training School established in Port-
    au-Prince in 1932.

VILLATTE.   Mulatto commander who sought unsuccess-
    fully to depose Toussaint L'Ouverture.

VINCENT, RENE.   Contemporary Haitian artist renowned
    for the psychological expressiveness of his painting.

VINCENT, STENIO.   A distinguished diplomat and jour-
    nalist who served as President of Haiti from 1930
    to 1941.   A mulatto and former mayor of Port-au-

Prince, he gained the presidency on the basis of
opposition to the U.S. occupation but became quite
pro-American after the U.S. withdrawal.
Vincent based his power on the Garde d'Haiti
and on officially-controlled plebiscites. He entered
office committed to the principle of parliamentary
government, but he became impatient with the legislature and asserted executive authority. The
Senate was declared "in rebellion to the will of the
people" in 1935 and its members expelled from the
chamber. He lost popularity as a result of his
partiality toward mulattoes and his weak reaction
to the Dominican massacre of Haitians in 1937.

VOLONTAIRES DE LA SECURITE NATIONALE   see
NATIONAL SECURITY VOLUNTEERS

VOODOO (also, vodou, vaudou, vodoun, vodon, vodun
and vaudoux). A term derived from the Dahomean
word meaning "spirit." Voodoo is a religion based
largely on West African beliefs and practices, including ancestor worship, the performance of pro-
pitiary rites, and belief in communication by trance
with dieties.
Voodoo purports to deal with the spirits by keeping the individual in harmonious relationship to
them. Worship is worked out in a complex ritual of
drawings, songs and dances, accompanied by the
drum, which is considered a sacred instrument.
It is said that Haitians are 90 percent Roman
Catholic and 100 percent voodoo adherents. Most
do not sense a contradiction between the two reli-
gions; in fact, a good deal of voodoo is incorpora-
ted into Christian practice in Haiti and vice versa.
There have been attempts to stamp out voodoo
in Haiti as a practice tending to perpetuate primitive mentality, but in view of its utility to the elite
in perpetuating their hold over the masses, it has
been condoned and even promoted by most govern-
ments. It is considered a tourist attraction, al-
though it should be noted that the voodoo as seen
by the tourist and the voodoo practiced in the back
country are two different things.

- W -

WANGA. According to voodoo belief, a charm that works
    malevolent magic.

WAR OF KNIVES. War between mulattoes, led by André
    Rigaud, and blacks, led by Toussaint L'Ouverture,
    1799-1800. Rigaud was defeated and fled to France.

WHIDDEN, BENJAMIN. First U. S. diplomatic represen-
    tative to Haiti. He came from New Hampshire and
    held the title of Commissioner.

WIENER, ODETTE. Organizer of Haitian folk-dance
    groups.

WINDWARD PASSAGE. The body of water separating
    Haiti from Cuba, called the U. S. gateway to the Carib-
    bean. The location of Haiti on the eastern side of the
    Windward Passage has given the country tremendous
    strategic importance. The passage is 1400 miles due
    south of New York and 900 miles northeast of the en-
    trance of the Panama Canal.

WORKER-FARMER MOVEMENT. A party formed by Dan-
    iel Fignolé in 1946. François Duvalier became its
    secretary-general.

- X -

XARAGUA (LE). Kingdom in the southwestern part of
    Hispaniola commanded by the Indian Chief Bohechio,
    with its capital Taguana, known today as Léogane.

- Y -

YAGUANA. Small village which later became known as
    Port-au-Prince. It was destroyed by the French
    pirate, François Le Clerc, in 1553.

YAM. A root vegetable of importance for human consumption and for voodoo rituals.

YANVALOU (Yenvalo) see AVALOU

- Z -

ZAMOR, ORESTE. President of Haiti for nine months in
   1914.

ZEME. God of the Indians who inhabited Haiti at the time
   of the island's discovery by Columbus.

ZEMI. A sacred object of the Arawak Indians who formerly
   inhabited Hispaniola.

'ZEPAULES. From "les epaules" (French, "shoulders").
   It refers to a voodoo ceremonial dance which accents
   shoulder movements.

Z'ILE MINFORT. An island below the water where the voodoo god, Agwé, is said to reside.

ZILET EN BAS DE L'EAU. An island below the sea
   where, according to voodoo belief, the souls of the
   dead are transported, and where a number of voodoo gods are said to reside.

ZIN. A pot used in the second stage of voodoo initia-
   tions. They were originally of iron and imported
   from Africa. Today they are more likely to be
   made of clay.

ZINGLINS. A quasi-military secret police set up by
   President (later Emperor) Soulouque in Port-au-
   Prince in the mid-19th century.

ZOMBIE. In Haiti, a dead person who has come to life,
   or someone so stupefied by drugs as to appear to
   be dead. In the first instance the person is said
   to have been resuscitated by a sorcerer whom he
   henceforth serves; in the second instance, a voodoo
   priest is said to have administered herbs to a person until that person fell into a coma. The "corpse"

is buried and later disinterred by the priest, who revives it; again the subject is said to be at his command.

Appendix

HAITIAN CHIEFS OF STATE

1804-1806	Jean Jacques Dessalines
1806-1820	Henri Christophe (north)
1806-1818	Alexandre Pétion (south)
1818-1843	Jean-Pierre Boyer
1843-1844	Charles Rivière Hérard, Ainé
1844-1845	Philippe Guerrier
1845-1846	Jean Louis Pierrot
1846-1847	Jean-Baptiste Riché
1847-1859	Faustin Soulouque
1859-1867	Fabre Nicolas Geffard
1867-1870	Sylvain Salnave
1870-1874	Nissage Saget
1874-1876	Michel Dominique
1876-1879	Boisrond Canal
1879-1888	Louis Etienne Félicité Lysius Salomon
1888-1889	François Denys Légitime
1889-1896	Florville Hyppolite
1896-1902	Tirésias Simon-Sam
1902-1908	Pierre Nord-Alexis
1908-1911	Antoine Simon
1911-1912	Cincinnatus Leconte
1912-1913	Tancrède Auguste

1913-1914	Michel Oreste
1914-1915	Oreste Zamor
1915	Davilmer Théodore
1915	Vilbrun Guillaume Sam
1915-1922	Philippe Sudre Dartinguenave
1922-1930	Louis Borno
1930-1941	Stenio Vincent
1941-1946	Elie Lescot
1946-1950	Dumarais Estimé
1950-1956	Paul E. Magloire
1956-1957	Nemours Pierre-Louis
1957	Franck Sylvain
1957	Daniel Fignolé
1957-1971	François Duvalier
1971-	Jean-Claude Duvalier

BIBLIOGRAPHIC ESSAY

The literature on Haiti is voluminous, though a good deal tends toward the romantic or the propagandistic. There is a dearth of objective, well-researched and well-documented analytical or factual material. Following is a general description of the most useful references, divided into five principal categories:

1. General sources
2. Bibliographies
3. History
   a. Spanish Colonial (1492-1697)
   b. French Colonial (Saint-Dominique) 1697-1791
   c. The Haitian Revolution (1791-1804)
   d. From Revolution to the U.S. Occupation (1804-1915)
   e. The U.S. Occupation (1915-1934)
   f. Modern-day Haiti (1934 to the present)
4. Economics
5. Culture

1. General Sources

There are few well-written general reference books on Haiti. The most recent and comprehensive volume is The Politics of Squalor (1971) by Robert I. Rotburg. Though not too sympathetic in its portrayal of the nation's history, it provides a good survey not only of the historical but also of the contemporary economic, cultural and political factors. Thomas E. Weil et al. 's Area Handbook for Haiti (1973), part of the series of country studies issued by the Foreign Area Studies office of the American University is broader in scope of subject matter (geography, history, social systems, living conditions, education, culture, public information, politics, economics and national security) but rather brief in the treatment of each of these subjects.

Two collections of papers have recently been published which are quite useful: The Haitian Potential (1975), edited by Vera Rubin and Richard Schaedel, and Working Papers in Haitian Society (1975), edited by Sidney W. Mintz. The first consists of sixteen papers dealing with such matters as demography, anthropology, sociology, community development, music, language, literacy, education, nutrition, public health, religion, psychiatry, institutions, labor and research. The collection by Mintz covers plantation society, post-revolutionary social structure, local government administration, marketing and bauxite mining.

2. Bibliographies

Scarecrow Press has published a dictionary of Haitian bibliography (Dictionnaire de bibliographie haitienne, Washington, D. C. , 1951). In addition, extensive general bibliographies can be found in Rotburg's The Politics of Squalor, Ott's The Haitian Revolution (1973) and the Area Handbook for Haiti (1973). The Rotburg and Ott volumes also carry useful bibliographic essays.

3. History

As general histories of Haiti, the following are most useful: Dantes Bellegarde's Histoire du Peuple Haitien, 1492-1952 (1953); J. N. Leger's Haiti, Her History and Her Detractors (1970); and Thomas Madiou's Histoire d'Haiti (1923) in three volumes. In addition, there are a number of useful references for the six principal periods in Haitian history:

a. Spanish Colonial

Perhaps the most valuable references to events on the island of Hispaniola during the period of Spanish domination are Sir James Barskett's History of the Island of St. Domingo: From its Discovery by Columbus (1818, repr. 1972); Dantes Bellegarde's Histoire du Peuple Haitien, 1492-1952 (1953); and Charlevoix's Histoire de l'Isle Espagnole ou de S. Dominique (1733) in four volumes.

b. French Colonial

The foremost work on pre-revolutionary Haiti is still Pierre de Vassière's Saint-Dominique (1906), though it shows considerable bias in favor of the white planters. Gwendolyn Hall's Social Control in Plantation Societies (1971) is also quite useful.

c. The Haitian Revolution

As one might expect, literature on the Haitian Revolution has been prolific and much of it has been written with a bias, running from C. J. R. James' Marxism to T. Lothrop Stoddard's white racism. Perhaps the most objective contemporary account was written by a British midshipman who was taken prisoner by Henri Christophe and later gained his favor: Marcus Rainsford (An Historical Account of the Black Empire of Haiti-pub. 1805, repr. 1972). Among recent books, Thomas Ott's The Haitian Revolution (1973) is probably the most authoritative.

Biographies of Haitian Revolutionary leaders have also appeared in great profusion, but they tend to be overly friendly and not too well researched, for example, Ann Griffiths' Black Patriot and Martyr (1970) on the life of Toussaint. A more thoughtful biography is Korngold's Citizen Toussaint (1965). Stephen Alexis' Black Liberator (1949) gives good insight on Toussaint's complex character, his rise to political power and his military campaigns. Cesaire Aimé's Toussaint aims at objectivity but is actually quite shallow in terms of research.

The best biography of a Haitian revolutionary hero

is Hubert Cole's Christophe (1967). In addition, Henry
Christophe and Thomas Clarkson: A Correspondence
(1952), by Griggs and Prator, is revealing of Christophe's
character, dreams and ambitions. In addition to carrying the texts of 60 letters written by the two men, Part
I of the book presents a superbly written history of Haiti
from 1492 to 1820. The only known biography of Dessalines is by Juan Lopez Cancelada.

d.   From Revolution to U. S. Occupation

This period, covering more than a century (1804
to 1915), is only lightly researched, and the most significant work has been done on the immediate post-revolutionary period.

The London firm of Frank Cass and Company,
Ltd., has reissued a number of superior works written
in English by diverse observers during the 19th century:

(1) Mark B. Bird, The Black Man (1969).
On mid-19th-century Haiti as seen through the eyes of
the republic's most energetic missionary. It is outstanding for its coverage of the Boyer presidency and
the reign of Emperor Faustin I.

(2) Jonathan Brown, The History and Present Condition of St. Domingo (1837, repr. 1972). The
best contemporary source on the reign of President Boyer, it also provides information on the rule of King
Christophe prior to 1820.

(3) John Candler, Brief Notices of Hayti
(1842, repr. 1972). An excellent contemporary account
of Haiti's critical first 40 years, written by a Quaker
missionary quite sympathetic to the young nation.

(4) James Franklin, The Present State of
Hayti (Saint Domingo) (1828, repr. 1972). Covers the
ethnology and material culture of early 19th-century Haiti, with some data on the structure of government.

(5) William Woodis Harvey, Sketches of

Hayti (1827, repr. 1972). On the revolution and its immediate aftermath. Together with Rainsford, he provides the best first-hand account of Christophe's rule.

(6) Mary Hassall, Secret History (1808, repr. 1972). Covers the campaigns of Le Clerc and Rochambeau and the rise of Toussaint, Dessalines and Christophe.

(7) Sir Spencer St. John, Hayti: Or, The Black Republic (1884; 1889). A critical account of voodoo and Haitian government practices by the British Consul in Haiti from about 1869 to 1879.

(8) Charles MacKenzie, Notes on Haiti (1830, repr. 1972). A personalized look at Haiti, 1826-1828, by another British consul.

Among more recently written books on the immediate post-revolutionary era Trouillot's Le Gouvernement du Roi Henri Christophe (1974) can be singled out as another sympathetic account of life in the magic kingdom of Henri Christophe.

Two other useful books spanning longer periods are James Leyburn's The Haitian People (1941, repr. 1966) and Ludwell Lee Montague's Haiti and the United States (1940), which, of course, has a special focus on Haiti-U.S. relations.

e.   The U.S. Occupation

The U.S. occupation of Haiti resulted in new and renewed interest in Haiti on the part of U.S. scholars. A number of critical books were written, the best being by Arthur C. Millspaugh, Hans Schmidt and Emily Greene Balch. Senator Paul H. Douglas of Illinois was in large part responsible for changes in U.S. policy toward Haiti during the occupation years, and his journal articles should be read for their revelations and courageous recommendations. Also, the Forbes Commission report on the U.S. occupation is basic reading.

f. Modern-day Haiti

Several books have recently appeared on contemporary Haiti, but most are heavily biased against the regime which was in power from 1957 to 1971. One example is Papa Doc (1969), an overdrawn, dramaticized account by two journalists, Al Burt and Bernard Diederich. Another devastating book, Graham Greene's The Comedians (1966), was made into a motion picture of the same name. Jean-Pierre Gingras' Duvalier, Caribbean Cyclone (1967), also falls in this category.

Among the more scholarly books written, the most outstanding are Leslie Manigat's Haiti of the Sixties (1964); Selden Rodman's Haiti: The Black Republic (1961); and Robert I. Rotberg's The Politics of Squalor (1971), all of which are critical but also generally fair in their criticism. François Duvalier's own work, Oeuvres Essentielles (2d ed., 1968), is valuable as an index to his political philosophy and mentality.

4. Economics

The best economic studies of Haiti (and for that matter most independent Latin American nations) are the so-called CIAP reports (country studies of the Inter American Committee on the Alliance for Progress), issued by the General Secretariat of the Organization of American States. However, these are internal documents, not generally available to the public.

In the public domain and almost as authentic, since the authors were economists with easy access to government data, are O. Ernest Moore's Haiti, Its Stagnant Society and Shackled Economy (1972); Edouard Francisque's Perspectives du Développement Economique en Haiti (1968); and Gerard Pierre-Charles' La economia haitiana y su via de desarollo (1965).

5. Culture

In the broad area of cultural affairs, scholarship

is also quite variable.   Voodoo is a favorite subject for
exploration--and for notorious distortion and misrepre-
sentation as well.   Sir Spencer St. John began the series
of exaggerated accounts of voodoo rites which extend to
the present day.

Among the most respected authors in the cultural
realm are Harold Courlander, Rémy Bastien, Jean Price-
Mars, Alfred Métraux and Katherine Dunham.   Price-
Mars has written prolifically in the field of ethnology and
linguistics.   Métraux and Dunham have done the most authoritative work on Haitian voodoo.   Miss Dunham, a
black anthropologist from Chicago, was herself actually
initiated into the second degree of the voodoo religion.
Edna Underwood's book on The Poets of Haiti (1935) is
also highly recommended.

Following is a highly selective list of one hundred
of the most useful titles with respect to Haiti and Haitian
life.   The selections are admittedly arbitrary, and many
commendable works have no doubt been overlooked.
Nevertheless, most of these titles would appear on most
experts' list of the most useful references for an introduction to Haitian life and manners.   Students interested
in Haitian affairs should not feel constrained by this list
but should explore also the titles found in the bibliographies cited at the head of this essay.

BIBLIOGRAPHY

Alexis, Stephen. Black Liberator: The Life of Toussaint L'Ouverture. William Sterling, trans. New York: Macmillan, 1949.

Balch, Emily Greene, ed. Occupied Haiti. New York: Writers Pub. Co., 1927.

Barskett, James. History of the Island of St. Domingo: From Its Discovery by Columbus. London: Frank Cass and Co., 1972 (reprint of 1818 ed.).

Bellegarde, Dantes. Ecrivains Haitiens. Port-au-Prince: Cheriqnit, 1948.

_____. Haiti et son peuple. Paris: Nouvelles Editions, 1953.

_____. Histoire du Peuple Haitien, 1492-1952. Port-au-Prince, 1953.

Bird, Mark B. The Black Man; or, Haytian Independence. London: Frank Cass and Co., 1969 (reprint, 1972).

Bonhomme, Colvert. Révolution et Contra-Révolution en Haiti de 1946 à 1947. Port-au-Prince, 1957.

Brand, William. Impressions of Haiti. The Hague, 1965.

Brown, Jonathan. The History and Present Condition of St. Domingo. London: Frank Cass and Co., 1972 (reprint of 1837 ed.).

Cancelada, Juan López. La vida de J. J. Dessalines.

Mexico City: Ontiveros, 1809.

Candler, John. Brief Notices of Hayti, with Its Conditions, Resources and Prospects. London: Frank
Cass and Co., 1972 (reprint of 1842 ed.).

Césaire, Aimé. Toussaint L'Ouverture: La Révolution
française et le probleme colonial. Paris: Le Club
Français du Livre, 1960.

Chapman, Charles E. "The Development of the Intervention in Haiti," The Hispanic American Historical Review, VII (1927) 299-319.

Charlevoix, Pierre-François Xavier de. Histoire de
l'Isle Espagnole ou de S. Dominique. Amsterdam,
1733, 4 vols.

Cole, Hubert. Christophe, King of Haiti. New York:
Viking, 1967.

Cooper, Donald B. "The Withdrawal of the United States
from Haiti, 1928-1934," Journal of Inter-American
Studies, V (1963) 83-101.

Courlander, Harold. The Drum and the Hoe: Life and
Lore of the Haitian People. Berkeley: University
of California Press, 1960.

_____ and Bastien, Rémy. Religion and Politics in
Haiti. Washington, D.C.: Institute of Cross Cultural Research, 1966.

Davis, H. P. Black Democracy: The Story of Haiti.
New York: Biblo and Tannen, 1967.

Debrien, Gabriel. Plantations et esclaves à Saint-Dominique. Daker, 1962.

Denis, Lorimer, and Duvalier, François. "La Civilisa-
tion Haitienne: Notre mentalité est-elle africaine
ou gallo-latine?" Revue de la Société d'Histoire et
de Géographic d'Haiti, VII (May, 1936) 1-31.

Bibliography   118

_____ and _____. Le Problème des classes à
travers l'histoire d'Haiti. Port-au-Prince, 1948 and
1958. (reprinted in Duvalier's Oeuvres Essentielles,
I, pp. 304-365.)

Diederich, Bernard, and Burt, Al. Papa Doc: The
Truth about Haiti Today. New York: McGraw-Hill,
1969.

Douglas, Paul H. "The American Occupation of Haiti,"
Political Science Quarterly, XLII (1927), 228-258,
368-396.

_____. "The National Railway of Haiti: A Study in
Tropical Finance," The Nation, CXXIV (19 Jan.
1927), 59-61.

Dunham, Katherine. Island Possessed. Garden City,
N.Y.: Doubleday, 1969.

Duvalier, François. Oeuvres Essentielles: I. Eléments
d'une Doctrine, 2d ed. Port-au-Prince, 1968.

Efron, Edith. "The 'New Movement' in Haiti," Caribbean Quarterly, IV (Jan. 1955), 14-31.

Elie, L. E. Histoire d'Haiti. Port-au-Prince, 1944-
1945, 2 vols.

Fagg, John. Cuba, Haiti and the Dominican Republic.
Englewood Cliffs, N.J.: Prentice-Hall, 1965.

Fermor, Patrick Leigh. The Traveller's Tree: A Jour-
ney Through the Caribbean Islands. London, 1950,
pp. 245-333.

Francisque, Edouard. Perspectives du développement
economique en Haiti. Port-au-Prince, 1968.

Franklin, James. The Present State of Hayti (Saint
Domingo). London: Frank Cass and Co., 1972 (reprint of 1828 ed.).

Gingras, Jean-Pierre O. Duvalier, Caribbean Cyclone:
The History of Haiti and Its Present Government.
New York: Exposition Press, 1967.

Gold, Herbert. The Age of Happy Problems. New York:
1962.

Greene, Graham. The Comedians. London, 1966.

Griffiths, Ann. Black Patriot and Martyr: Toussaint of
Haiti. New York: Julian Messner, 1970.

Griggs, Earl, and Prator, Clifford, eds. Henry Christophe and Thomas Clarkson: A Correspondence.
Berkeley: University of California Press, 1952.

Hall, Gwendolyn. Social Change in Plantation Societies:
A Comparison of St. Dominique and Cuba. Baltimore: Johns Hopkins Press, 1971.

Harvey, William Woodis. Sketches of Hayti--From the
Expulsion of the French to the Death of Christophe.
London: Frank Cass and Co., 1972 (reprint of 1827
ed.).

Hassall, Mary. Secret History, or the Horrors of St.
Domingo. London: Frank Cass and Co., 1972 (reprint of 1808 ed.).

Herskovits, Melville J. Life in a Haitian Valley. New
York: Octagon Books, 1964.

Hoetink, Harry. "Over de sociaal-raciale structuur van
Haiti," Tijdschrift van het Koninklyk Nederlandsch
Aardrykskundig Genootschap (Netherlands) vol. 78,
no. 2 (1961), 146-156.

Huxley, Francis. The Invisibles. London, 1966.

Inter American University of Puerto Rico. The Caribbean in Crisis: Cuba, Haiti and the Dominican Republic. San German, P.R.: Caribbean Institute and
Study Center for Latin America, 1965.

James, C. L. R. The Black Jacobins, 2d ed. New
      York: Vintage Books, 1963.

Jelliffe, Derrick B., and E. F. Patricia, "The Nutri-
      tional Status of Haitian Children," Acta Tropica,
      XVII, 1 (1961), 1-45.

Korngold, Ralph. Citizen Toussaint, 2d ed. New York:
      Hill, 1965.

Leger, J. N. Haiti, Her History and Her Detractors.
      Westport, Conn.: Negro Universities Press, 1970.

Lepelletier de Saint-Rémy, R. Saint-Dominique: Etude
      et solution nouvelle de la question haitienne. Paris,
      1846.

Lepkowski, Tadeusz. Haiti: Poczatki Panstwa i Narodu
      [Haiti: The Beginning of the State and the Nation].
      Warsaw, 1964.

Leyburn, James G. The Haitian People. New Haven,
      Conn.: Yale University Press, 1941 (reissued, 1966).

_____. "The Making of a Black Nation," in George
      Peter Murdock, ed., Studies in the Science of So-
      ciety, New Haven, 1937, 377-394.

Loederer, Richard. Voodoo Fire in Haiti. London,
      1935.

Logan, Rayford W. The Diplomatic Relations of the
      United States with Haiti, 1776-1891. Chapel Hill:
      University of North Carolina Press, 1941.

_____. Haiti and the Dominican Republic. New York:
      Oxford University Press, 1968.

MacKenzie, Charles. Notes on Haiti. London: Frank
      Cass and Co., 1972 (reprint of 1830 ed.).

Madiou, Thomas. Histoire d'Haiti, 2d ed. Port-au-
      Prince: Département de l'Instruction Publique, 1922-
      1923, 3 vols.

Manigat, Leslie F. Haiti of the Sixties: Object of International Concern. Washington, D.C., 1964.

Métral, Antoine. Histoire de l'insurrection des esclaves
dans le nord de Saint-Dominique. Paris, 1818.

Métraux, Alfred. Haiti: Black Peasants and Voodoo.
Peter Legnyel, trans. New York: Schocken Books,
1960.

_____. Voodoo in Haiti. New York: Schocken Books,
1959.

Millspaugh, Arthur C. Haiti under American Control,
1915-1930. Boston: World Peace Foundation, 1931.

Mintz, Sidney W., ed. Working Papers in Haitian Society and Culture. New Haven, Conn. : Yale University, 1975.

Montague, Ludwell Lee. Haiti and the United States,
1714-1938. Durham, N.C.: Duke University Press,
1940.

Moore, O. Ernest. Haiti, Its Stagnant Society and
Shackled Economy. New York: Exposition Press,
1972.

Munro, Dana. "The American Withdrawal from Haiti,
1929-1934," Hispanic American Historical Review,
XLIX, no. 1 (Feb. 1969), 1-26.

Ott, Thomas C. The Haitian Revolution, 1789-1804.
Knoxville: The University of Tennessee Press, 1973.

Pierre-Charles, Gérard. La economía haitiana y su via
de desarolla. Mexico City, 1965.

Poyen, H. de. Histoire militaire de la Révolution de
Saint-Dominique. Paris: Berger-Levrault, 1899.

Price-Mars, Jean. Ainsi parla l'oncle: Essais d'eth-
nographie. Comiègne, France, 1928.

Rainsford, Marcus. An Historical Account of the Black
    Empire of Hayti. London: Frank Cass and Co.,
    1972 (reprint of 1805 ed.).

Rodman, Selden. "Artistas de Haiti," Americas, XX,
    no. 10. (Oct. 1968), 8-15.

_____. Haiti: The Black Republic. New York: De-
    vin-Adair, 1961.

Rotberg, Robert I. The Politics of Squalor: The Evo-
    lution and Development of Modern Haiti. Boston:
    Houghton-Mifflin Co., 1971.

Rubin, Vera, and Schaedel, Richard, eds. The Haitian
    Potential: Research and Resources of Haiti. New
    York: Teachers College, 1975.

St. John, Spencer. Hayti, or the Black Republic. New
    York, 1889.

Schmidt, Hans. The U.S. Occupation of Haiti, 1915-
    1934. New Brunswick, N.J.: Rutgers University
    Press, 1971.

Schoelcher, Victor. Vie de Toussaint L'Ouverture, 2d
    ed. Paris, 1889.

Seabrook, W. B. The Magic Island. New York, 1929.

Sebrell, W. H., Jr., et al. "Appraisal of Nutrition in
    Haiti," American Journal of Clinical Nutrition, VII
    (1959).

Simpson, George Eaton. "Haitian Politics," Social
    Forces XX (1942), 487-491.

Steedman, Mabel. Unknown to the World; Haiti. Lon-
    don, 1939.

Stoddard, T. Lothrop. The French Revolution in Santo
    Domingo. Boston: Houghton, 1914.

Streit, Clarence K. "Haiti: Intervention in Operation, "
Foreign Affairs VI (1928), 615-632.

Stycos, J. Mayone. "Haitian Attitudes Toward Family
Size, " Human Organization XXIII, No. 1 (1964),
42-47.

Taft, Edna. A Puritan in Voodoo-Land. Philadelphia,
1934.

Thomas, Lowell. Old Gimlet Eye: The Adventures of
Smedley D. Butler as told to Lowell Thomas. New
York, 1933.

Trouillot, Henock. Le Gouvernement du Roi Henri
Christophe. Port-au-Prince: Imprimerie Centrale,
1974.

Underwood, Edna W. The Poets of Haiti. Portland,
Maine: The Master Press, 1935.

Vaissière, Pierre de. Les Origins de la Colonisation
et la Formulation de la Société Française à Saint-
Dominique. Paris, 1906.

_____. Saint-Dominique: La Société et la vie creole
sous l'Ancien Régime (1629-1789). Paris: Perrin,
1909.

Vastey, Baron de. An Essay on the Causes of the Revolution and Civil Wars of Hayti. London: Western
Luminary Office, 1823.

Waxman, Percy. The Black Napoleon. New York: Har-
court, 1931.

Weil, Thomas E. , et al. Area Handbook for Haiti.
Washington, D. C. : U. S. Gov. Printing Office, 1973.

Wilson, Ruth Danenhower. Here Is Haiti. New York,
1957.

Wimpffen, François Alexandre Stanislaus Baron de. A

Voyage to Saint-Domingo in the Years 1788, 1789 and 1790. J. Wright, trans. London, 1817.

Wirkus, Faustin E., and Dudley, Taney. The White King of La Gonâve. Garden City, N. Y. : Doubleday, 1931.